WHO'S IN YOUR CIRCLES AND WHY?

"Who's in Your Circles and Why," will quickly become a powerful classic that will be appreciated time and time again for many years to come. This wonderful self-help and empowerment book superbly explores and amplifies the important dynamics of communication in human relationships. The author makes brilliant use of "Once upon a time, in a land far, far away." This inimitable style coalesced with potent psychological principles and the author's many years of experience, gives birth to what will surely become a standard. With enchanting lands and planets of mystery as the backdrop for this amazing voyage; from cover to cover you are simply riveted and glued to each and every page, as you take a journey into the AMAZING LANDS OF CIRCLES.

Dr. (Colonel) Gilmer Hayes

"I could not put this book down."   Ms. Melanie Cummings

I did not have to read this book to know that it was going to be empowering. After all, I know the author. However, after reading the book, I now feel that I know him just a little bit better. I would buy this book, even if he was not my husband. ☺

Dr. Evelyn Harper-Alberty

Dr. J. Calvin Alberty's

EMPOWERMENT, COMMUNICATION, AND SELF-HELP BOOK

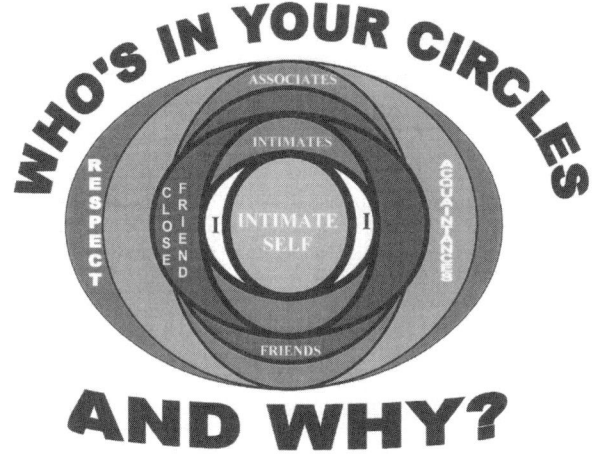

First Edition

Gracewood, Georgia

**DR. J. CALVIN ALBERTY'S
EMPOWERMENT, COMMUNICATION AND SELF-HELP BOOK**

HOW TO TAKE CONTROL OF YOUR LIFE FOREVER

WIJAH Publishing Company, LLC
P. O. BOX 82
GRACEWOOD, GA 30812 U.S.A.
www.whosinyourcircles.com

Unattributed quotations are by Dr. J. Calvin Alberty

First Edition ISBN 978-0-9800181-0-3

Printed in the United States of America

Library of Congress Cataloging-in-Publication Data

Alberty, John
Who's In Your Circles and Why, Excuse Me, What Did You Say? / by Dr. John Alberty. – 1st ed.

Includes bibliographical references
ISBN-13: 978-0-9800181-0-3

Cover image designed by Dr. J. Calvin Alberty

Contents

CHAPTER	TITLE	PAGE
	About The Author	7
	Acknowledgement	8
	Dedication	9
	Warnings and Disclaimers	10
	Preface	11
	A Limerick from the Lands of Circles	15
1	The Meeting	17
2	The Journey	27
3	The First Circle	41
4	Into the First Circle	51
5	The Land of Acquaintances	73
6	A Whole New Land	91
7	Lessons From the Special Ones	127
8	Further Lessons From the Special Ones (Remember the Butterfly)	145
9	Lessons on the Circles	155
10	A Lesson in the Trees	165
11	A Major Lesson on a Circle beyond the Circles	171
12	How and Why People Make the Choices They Make	193
13	Going Deeper to Understand the Strings	213

Contents Continued

CHAPTER	TITLE	PAGE
14	Back to the Lands of Circles	219
15	We All Start Out Winners	221
16	We Are Unique	227
17	The Dark Experience on the Planet Odium AKA the Planet Loveless	239
18	The Words of Wisdom	251
19	The Universe and Confusion	257
20	Another Lesson in the Path	267
21	It Did Not Start That Way	277
22	Prelude to a Dark Activity that Must Never Enter Any Circle	295
23	A Quick Lesson on Circles	297
24	The Darkest Circle	301
25	The Amazing Circle of Planets	317
26	Another Name for the Lands of Circles	327
27	A Poignant Departure	335
28	You Haven't Seen Anything Yet (Quick Tips From the Special Ones)	339
	References	351
	Appendix	353

About the Author

Dr. Alberty is a Licensed Professional Counselor in the State of Georgia. He also holds the following certifications: Nationally Certified Counselor; Master Addiction Counselor; and Clinically Certified Juvenile Treatment Speicalist. He holds a doctorate (Ed.D.) in Counseling Psychology as well as a Ph.D. in Nutrition from a holistic perspective.

He began his career in counseling psychology in 1975 as a crisis intervention specialist. It was baptism by fire, but he learned a great deal that would inspire his love for counseling, and crisis-based counseling caused him to learned it quickly. He has a deep concern for the welfare and well-being of others. He believes that the potential for greatness lies within each of us.

He defines adversities as stepping stones on a path called growth; and excuses as stumbling blocks on a path to nowhere. He dedicates himself to the belief that every soul has value. Dr. Alberty loves empowering others to discover the greatness within themselves. His greatest joy is witnessing the epiphanies that others experience in the discovery and realization of their greatness.

He has authored several books. He is a poet, author, and motivational speaker. He finds happiness in his marriage of 34 years, his family, and that rare breed called true friends. He has poured his heart and soul into this book, and desires only that you will learn from it; tell others about it, and enjoy its benefits to the utmost.

Acknowledgement

I would like to acknowledge the inspiration that others have given. I am indebted to my wife Evelyn for the great comittment that she demonstrated in seeing this book through to the end and inspiring me with her love each step of the way. I recognize the importance of my mother, Dorothy Burton, her encouragement and belief knew no bounds. Her love is unconditional. I am aware of the future challenges for little Jay and Jordan. This, along with my love for Kim, John, James, and Corey motivates me to work through the tiredness.

I acknowledge that the most important factor in making this book possible has been the love of an awesome God. He is a God who specializes in making a way out of no way. I appreciate Dr. (Colonel) Hayes, as a mentor for his wisdom and focus on getting the job done. Thanks to Elizabeth Lewis who loved me when I needed it most, and Vincent, who taught me laughter. I acknowledge the continued encouragement from Carolyn, whose love for young people have changed so many lives for the better. I thank Jay and Betty for their support.

I want to commend Henry Nash for his amazing achievements that continue to inspire me. I give recognition and thanks to Alfred, Arthur, and Robert for their accomplishments and their belief in the bond of brotherhood. I thank Johnny for loving Veo like the brother he is. To Mitch, I salute you. To Cornelius, and Jimmy, I love you. Those were some amazing days, where we were the strength for each other. Kenneth, Otis and Norman, I will never forget you. Fnally, to the memory of those that my heart long for and that I truly miss: Mack, Bennie, Dwight, Maurice, Wayne, and Roderick; we all love you.

Dedication

This book is dedicated to every individual who will gather strength and courage from the inspiring truths upon its pages, and who will exercise the power within their hearts to embrace them. I applaud you for caring enough about yourselves to invest in your well-being this day, with this book. I truly believe that there is an amazing power for change within each of us. What you think matters. Who you are matters. Your life is pregnant with seeds of greatness that only need your belief to be fertilized.

I challenge you to believe in the greatness within you. I dare you to follow your dreams; to live out your visions; and to ignore the voices of the naysayers that are merely the pusillanimous echoes of their own fears. You began life as a winner. As children your minds were fertile with dreams, excited by possibilities, and looked forward to the day that you would accomplish each of them. You are somebody! More than that, you are somebody with unlimited potential that pleads to be realized.

I dedicate this book to your growth. I dedicate it to your finding within these pages and within yourself, the voice of that little child that cries in frustration. It cries because it knows of the greatness within you. It believes that you can do anything that you put your mind to; and that you are willing to work for as though your life depended on it. I dedicate this book to greatness! I dedicate this book to success! I dedicate this book to unlimited possibilities. I dedicate this book to that very special person in whom all of these qualities can be found. I dedicate this book to YOU!

9

Warnings and Disclaimers

This book is designed to present information on communicating in a manner that empowers and liberates the reader. It is sold with the understanding that the publisher and author are not engaged in rendering advice for your unique and personal situation. You must use good judgment in assessing your personal situation and what works best for you.

It is the intention of this book to complement, augment and enhance other readings on empowerment that you might have read or studied. You are urged to read multiple authors and converse with those that you highly respect, if appropriate, and tailor the information to your unique and personal needs.

Empowerment is a process that begins with a made up mind. You must assess that you are not happy where you are and become determined to do something about it. You cannot finish what you do not start. This book makes recommendations that could empower you forever. However, recommendations are like pills. Some are good for you, some will not alter anything, and some could have negative consequences. If you are in a situation that has become unbearable, I also recommend professional counseling.

This text should be used only as a general guide and not to replace common sense and wisdom. The purpose of this book is to educate with a knowledge that leads to wise decisions and positive outcomes. The author and WIJAH Publishing Company, LLC shall have no liability or responsibility to any person or entity with respect to any loss or damage caused, or alleged to have been caused, directly or indirectly, by the information contained in this book.

PREFACE

If you possess the wisdom, intellect, or even the curiosity to purchase this book, you are about to embark upon a vicarious, and yet very real journey, that could alter your life forever! The incorporation and implementation of these phenomenal concepts, practices and principles in your life will give you power and control in your relationships rarely experienced by others.

These concepts will immensely diminish the exposure to vulnerability that too many of us encounter in our relationships with others. Imagine, forever ridding your life of the limiting and destructive patterns of social and intimate interactions that have kept you from moving forward and caused you to live your life with a considerable number of regrets. Even now, you must know that it is time for you; yes for YOU to take control of your life and demand respect from the people in it.

This book has begged to be written over eons and ages. It has finally manifested itself for such a time as this and for such a person as you. It is not an accident that you are now holding this powerful resource for change in your hand. Surely, when you read this book you will recognize truths and revelations for which your soul has longed and yearned. You will hear yourself saying, "I knew that, so why haven't I put it into practice?"

Some of the major pieces of this magnificent puzzle that we call life will finally come together with a clarity never before realized. You will honestly see that it is "how and where" we communicate and interact with others, within the

11

circles of communication, (yet to be explained) that either binds us or frees us. I trust that you will see these concepts of interpersonal relationships, relative to interpersonal communication, from an entirely different perspective.

You will understand that the way others view and perceive us, is directly related to the "who, what, when, where, why, and how" of communication. If you had already read this amazing book, you would know exactly what this means. The specificity and clarity with which these concepts are presented will put forward a mandate for change. This book will inspire you to set boundaries for how you interact with others and how you permit others to interact with you.

I truly believe that this is like no other book that you have ever read. These writings emanate from an effervescent pool of passion that has compelled Dr. Alberty to write from the perspective of one who has enjoyed both the art and science of counseling psychology for more than twenty years. Before becoming a Licensed Professional Counselor in the State of Georgia, or obtaining a Doctorate in Counseling Psychology, or even obtaining his Nationally Certified Counselor's status, many individuals and couples presented issues to him that were serious threats to their relationships. These issues were often the result of **malcommunication**.

Before delving into the rich preventative, curative, and healing atmosphere of this book, we must clearly define this term identified as malcommunication. It is a term which reflects one or more of the shameful seven violations of communication. And to define it we must look closely at the etymology, or history of the prefix "mal." It is from Old French meaning **bad, abnormal or**

inadequate. I would like to also give it a meaning that equates to the word **"wrong."**

Therefore, as you read this book and encounter anything that can be conceptualized as: 1) bad communication; 2) abnormal communication; 3) inadequate communication; 4) wrong communication; 5) miscommunication, 6) poor communication, or 7) the lack of communication, consider it one of these shameful seven methods of malcommunication.

The uniqueness of this book will soon become apparent, as it is steep with lessons that will easily reach out and grab hold of your heart; and I assure you that you will indeed learn lessons that will forever leave an indelible imprint in your soul. However, we can not learn these lessons here in this present sphere that we call earth. I must invite you to embark upon an inspiring journey with me to an ancient, obscure, and unfrequented land of which few mortals are aware. It is wonderful utopia called the "Lands of Circles."

Instead of merely telling you about it, you are allowed to take a vicarious and sensational journey with me, back through the annals of time, or maybe it is forward, or it could even be in a parallel dimension or continuum of time. Open your mind, and journey as I have, to experience the wonders of these mysterious and wonderful lands for yourself. These are lands that are munificent with their wisdom. If you are an assiduous and persevering traveler to and through these lands that have no paragon, your mind will be elevated, and I assure you that your world will never again be the same.

WHO'S IN YOUR CIRCLES

Surely, as you approach the close of your journey from these enriching and enchanting Lands of Circles, you will take control and mastery of your life as never before. This control will emerge as you begin to clearly understand the answer to the title question, "Who's in your circles and why?" And you will enthusiastically proclaim that you have never been so empowered and invigorated for positive change in all of your life! Now come with me as we begin our magnificent voyage deep into the unspoiled and pristine utopia that I call the Lands of Circles.

BUT FIRST, A LITTLE LIMERICK FROM THESE VERY LANDS

<u>A Limerick from the Lands of Circles</u>

You may think that this tale is not true
So you say, but my friend if you knew
It's as true as can be
It's alive and so free
And once read with your heart you'll be too.

WHO'S IN YOUR CIRCLES

CHAPTER ONE
The Meeting

Our voyage begins at the end of a very long, arduous, and

exacting day. My overtaxed mind aches to be delivered from the

bondage in which it is held by the mounds of paperwork that are

anchored to my desk demanding to be completed. Outside, the sun

loses its fight for dominance as the shadows of the evening sky

unrelentingly force it beneath a starry blanket of darkness. A waxing

gibbous moon glows with a personal invitation for me to escape the

confine of my office. However, continually and incessantly screaming

from my desk is a stagnant mound of records. They are insisting that

I cannot leave. They have taken on the role of my personal

antagonist. So as I sit in my not-so-easy, easy-chair, pondering the

dubiousness of my plight, a tall, bearded, and fashionably dressed

stranger suddenly appears outside my door.

Several years ago it became my custom to lock the outer office

door after meeting with my last scheduled client of the day.

Fortunately, today had not been an exception. My attention however,

was arrested by the rapidity and intensity of the stranger's determined

pounding against the thick glass panes of the door. It was a "let me in now" knock, rather than an "I am waiting at your door" knock. They were "stressful, worrying, distressing, and almost traumatic" blows. They demanded entrance, rather than softly tapping and rapping and cordially requesting entrance.

Initially startled and surprised; maybe even frightened, I sat motionless. I was glued to my chair with my eyes firmly fastened on the intense and persistent stranger. I was straining in my hurried effort to quickly, yet thoroughly assess him. His posture and demeanor reflected a sort of unsettled anxiousness. He had a restless look in his eyes. Yet, for a surety, there was a very overt and perceptible air of dignity about him. It was a dignity that to some extent allayed my fears, while simultaneously heightening my curiosity.

The front of my office suite was fully glassed. It was a kind of double insulated glass that was very darkly tinted. Even the office door was included. Normally, I could see out of the glass, but those outside could not see in. However, I strongly suspected that this man could see me. The origin of this suspicion eluded me. However, I learned to trust that still small voice that had so many times correctly spoken to me in the past.

As I sat there wondering, he pounded against the door again, but this time with even more determination. Now his fist exploded against the door as though it was filled with a stick of dynamite. He now seemed to stare not only in my direction, but directly into my eyes. There was now a definitive certainty on my part that he could see me. His intensity of knocking was equaled only by the deep seated intensity of my consternation and trepidation. Hesitantly, and I mean very hesitantly, I arose from the chair and slowly approached the door with measured and deliberate steps.

Why I felt so compelled to unlock the door eluded me. Yet, as though they were disconnected from my brain, my feet rebelliously shuffled their way toward the door when everything within me was ferally screaming a definitive NO. He immediately pushed his way in. He did so in an abrupt and firm manner. He failed to make an introduction of himself, as he "demanded" more than "asked," "Are you Dr. Ambrose?" There was urgency in his every move and word. He asked as though he already knew the answer to the question being asked of me.

Innately, I paused before answering, "Yes, yes I am, and you are?" My answer had purposely been slow and deliberate.

"As you will soon discover Dr. Ambrose, who I am, is not an important matter; not important at all." He retorted. "But what I have to tell you is very significant." He stated with great emphasis on the word "what." "May I have a seat?" He inquired, despite the fact that he sat before I could answer him. "You're probably wondering who I am, more than what my name is, and certainly you are asking yourself even now, what is my purpose for being here? Frankly I don't blame you."

Returning to my seat, I was more confused now than when he stood outside the office door. He continued, "As I said, my name is truly not of importance; not of importance at all, but my mission is extremely so." He stated strongly stressing the latter few words. "I have been sent..."

"Mission? Sent?" I interjected abruptly, "By whom and why? You may not think that your name is important, but for starters, I would really like to know who I am speaking to. And furthermore . . ."

In an even more frustrated tone than that of my own, he interjected, "In time Dr. Ambrose, in time, but right now you must understand that these are questions that I am neither prepared, nor privileged to answer at the present moment. I am only a messenger on a mission. I was instructed to personally present you with what is simply a most unique and exceptional opportunity."

I was beginning to assess the stranger as someone with a serious mental problem. Yet I must admit, that at least for the moment, he did have my full and undivided attention.

"Why do you look at me like that Dr. Ambrose? I am not a mad man." He stressed as though he had read my mind. "And as I have told you, this is indeed a most unique and exceptional opportunity with which you are being presented."

My response was filled with sarcasm and cynicism, "Unique and exceptional huh?"

"Indeed it is. Once a year they send me out in search of someone like you."

"They? Who are they and what do you mean someone like me?" As I was about to ask him to leave, he continued.

"Dr. Ambrose, you must listen to me." He insisted as he very deliberately stressed his enunciation of the word must. "These questions will answer themselves. I am not presently allowed to answer them, but only to do as I have been precisely directed. Now please allow me to continue. Once a year they send me out to some designated person, to whom I am privileged to present with what I personally know to be the opportunity of many lifetimes."

Pulling a large envelope from his inner suit pocket and placing it on the desk in front of me, he stares unflinchingly into my eyes without uttering another word. "What is this?" I asked, almost afraid of the answer.

"Now, that Dr. Ambrose is a question that I can answer." He smiled for the first time. "It is several pages of directions that will guide you on a journey that will live in your heart forever, should you choose to accept it. Go ahead and read the first page." He provocatively challenged.

After carefully looking at the document resting in front of me atop my files, I finally picked it up. Turning to the first page, I saw exactly what you will see below.

Board the 7:00 AM flight at gate 45, from Hartsfield-Jackson Atlanta International Airport to . . .

"To where, is what you're wondering." He stated as though he was a clairvoyant or seer. "Go ahead and turn to the next page."

As I attempted to do so, I soon discovered that the pages were by some means bonded together and could not be separated. "What's going on?" I blurted.

He smiled again, somewhat deviously and said, "The pages will separate and allow you to view the following page only after you have accomplished what you have read on the preceding page." I was discovering that he purposely gave strong emphasis to certain words as he spoke. This time the word emphasized was "after". "Therefore, the next page will be released when you reach the Atlanta airport, approximately ninety minutes before your flight is scheduled to depart. And by the way, whatever you might do, do not lose these instructions. For the present time, you simply read what you can and the rest will be revealed to you as you successfully complete each task; or shall I say, as needed."

Once again I turned my attention to the papers that he had given to me. Over and over again, I read the incomplete statement saying, "Board the 7:00 AM flight at gate 45 from Hartsfield-Jackson Atlanta International Airport to . . ." I continually queried and battered myself with one question after the other. "Who is this man? Why me? Why now? Where to?" My mind was boiling in turmoil, and in my frustration I cried out, "How can I accomplish this? How can I board a 7:00 AM flight from Atlanta when I don't know the, date, carrier, destination or anything?"

It was then that I noticed his extended hand with several plane tickets. One was a dated ticket from Atlanta departing at 7:00 AM. Before I could ask the next question, the stranger abruptly stood to his feet and quickly made his way to the door.

"It is really quite simple Dr. Ambrose. Are you adventurous or not? Will you pass up this glorious opportunity to alter your life forever? And not just your life Dr. Ambrose, but the lives of millions that will forever be altered for the better when you write your memoirs of this remarkable experience? If you accept, this whole excursion will take only a few weeks of your time. If you choose not to accept, do not be overly concerned; the documents have an intelligence of their own and will only be usable when your hands are on them at their exact designated geographical locations. Otherwise, they will remain blank for a short while, and then suddenly vanish. You know, poof, like smoke into thin air, disappear, poof."

"This is ridiculous." I declared, as I tried to convince myself of the pure craziness of this entire situation.

"Yes, perhaps it is crazy, even ridiculous." He said while leaning in close to my face and continuing with these words, "But is it just crazy and ridiculous enough for you to take the journey?" A broad smile crept slowly across his countenance, as he confidently placed the black derby on top of his head and exited my office. I rushed to the door to call after him, but no one was there. It was as if he had literally disappeared.

I hurriedly locked the office door and quickly returned to my seat. I sat there alone running every word that the stranger had spoken through my head over and over, again and again. But with all of my mental efforts, there was still little to no clarity forthcoming. I had come closer to convincing myself that to take this trip would be ludicrous. I threw the tickets along with their directions into the wastebasket beside my desk. For the next hour, I sat there, glued to my chair in a surreal and altered state of mind. I was almost catatonically staring at the wastebasket. I was overwhelmed, and at times I was enthralled in a desperate struggle between curiosity and common sense. I strained my brain, almost bursting blood vessels in an effort to make sense of how the events of the evening had unfolded. The thought, "What do I have to lose?" was the theme of the broken record that was repetitively playing its twisted discourse within my mind. It was a logic that my powers of reasoning could not refute or gainsay. I remembered the words of Dr. Aye, my favorite professor of many years ago. "He who races ahead of reason runs in the company of fools." Just as I had finally talked myself out of taking the trip, I had just as easily convinced myself that it would be even more ludicrous and foolish not to take it.

CHAPTER TWO
The Journey

Five taxies, six planes, two trains, one bus and two ferries later, I found myself standing in a fog, both literally and figuratively. It was a very strange place, on what had now already revealed itself as an even stranger journey. The man was correct; the directions given to me had revealed themselves one page at a time upon my arrival at each new destination. I now found myself standing on a small pier that rocked and creaked with the ebb and flow of each tide. In the distance I could hear a fog horn and what appeared to be a buoy bell.

Through the thick oppressive fog, which blinded me to all but my immediate surroundings, I could at least determine that the area was heavily foliaged with tropical plants that were rooted in what appeared to be dark rich soil. It was a humid environment, alive with the sounds of various birds; and only God knew what the other sounds were. Strangely in spite of the thick fog, as I squatted low with one knee on the pier, I could see right to the bottom of the crystal clear water that lapped unceasingly against the pier. And though obscured by the haze, I could sense that the sun was quickly beginning to sink. It was descending behind what appeared to be the barely perceptible broken outlines of towering and jagged mountains; mountains that were casting their eerie shadows over my haunting, mysterious, and enigmatic surroundings.

Absent of any warning, I heard the discernable sound of someone clearing their throat. It was the forgotten cab driver; forgotten because I was so caught up with the mystique of this place that nothing else seemed to matter. He was forgotten because my thoughts were held prisoner, by what was ahead of me rather than what or who was behind me. My inner voice screamed, what in the world possessed me to come here? Again, he cleared his throat. Already I had generously paid him extra to wait with me until my contact person arrived. I made my way to him through the fog to be greeted by his extended hand indicating the obvious. As I once again reached into my pocket, I appealed to him not to leave.

"Here's an extra twenty for waiting." I offered, in my effort to insure that I had a way to get back to wherever I had come from. At that very moment a boat pulled up to the pier. Immediately I heard the sputtering engine of the cab fading as the dense fog engulfed its tail lights along with my twenty-dollar bill.

After being unceremoniously abandoned by the driver I turned back toward the pier to hear only two words spoken, "Get in." I clumsily stepped into the small boat almost turning it over. The drive to this point by the cabbie had seemingly taken forever, and he had only spoken maybe two words at the most. Now it appeared that the operator of the boat was going to be even worse. He never once turned to face me, as he grunted taciturnly, "Sit down."

The boat was propelled by what appeared to be a small trolling engine. It was precariously mounted in an odd makeshift manner onto the rear of the boat with several cords and wires. It was now late evening, somewhere between dusk and dark. As the boat finally pulled away from the pier we were greeted with a thickening fog that engulfed us into its blinding bowels. The visibility was now zero. Though I was the lone passenger on this meandering vessel, fear and trepidation were my unwelcomed and ever present companions. The single operator, barely acknowledging my presence, did absolutely nothing to comfort me.

"Excuse me sir." I called out, after struggling to gather the courage to get the operator's attention. "But I never told you where I was going."

"Did you tell the cab driver where you were going?" He retorted.

After a brief pause, I was shocked to hear myself saying, "No, no I did not."

"Only one place to go from here." He tersely mumbled, while still not bothering to look toward me. The fog was now so thick that I could not see him or my own hand moving in front of my face. I was cramped and uncomfortable, but I did not contemplate moving for fear of falling out of the narrow canoe-like vessel. And I was also afraid to imagine what might be lurking in the waters beneath us.

Once again I attempted to make conversation. As crazy as it sounds, I wanted to make sure that I was not suddenly alone in the boat. I had reached a point where I was wary of everything. "How often do you take passengers to this place?" I questioned above the quiet puttering of the engine.

"Once a year." He answered. From the sound of his voice he was continuing to stare ahead, almost refusing to look toward me. I comforted myself with the thought, that had he turned around, he would not have been able to see me with the thickness of the fog. But that thought was secondary to the fear that assaulted my mind as

I suddenly thought that we might crash into something at any moment; after all, how could he see?

I felt that he sensed my discomfort as I strained to engage him in conversation. "There doesn't appear to be much competition for passengers." I nervously laughed.

"There is none. This is the only boat that travels these waters, and this is the one time yearly that we are allowed through these narrow and perilous channels. The fog is the land's natural blindfold designed to not only obscure our sense of direction, but any landmarks that might serve to guide us here again."

"Wait a minute." I thought to myself before blurting out. "The engine is back here. How do you steer it from up there with no steering mechanism?"

"The answer is simple. I don't. I too am a passenger. The motor is alive and has intelligence like everything else does in this land. But you need not worry, I have never lost a passenger; and there is no other way to reach the amazing Lands of Circles."

"Is that my destination?" I asked, but received no answer. After a brief and awkward pause, I continued, "You are the first person to really tell me anything. I really don't have a clue as to why or what I am doing here."

I was quickly reaching the apex of complete exasperation, which only exacerbated the tenuous and unstable condition of my already fragile state of mind. Suddenly, without warning, rhyme or reason, the fog instantaneously lifted like a giant theatrical curtain being raised. My eyes were suddenly witnessing the most beautiful and enchanting paradise ever imaginable.

In the distance, a solitary figure stood waving from the beach. The blood seemed to suddenly rush from my upper torso as I noticed that I was in the boat alone. I felt faint as I listened to the hum of the engine, which inexplicably idled itself down as it guided the boat to shore where the stranger stood waving. As I screamed within myself over the absence of the captain, another part of me screamed, "It's him!" It was the man from my office; the very one who had presented me with the package and tickets.

"Your questions will soon begin to find their own answers Dr. Ambrose." He smiled as he took my hand and helped me from the boat. "However, you must still exercise patience, as you and I are now about to enter the wonders of the Lands of Circles. Remember, we are both guests and observers. This means that we will only be able to observe in these lands that we are entering. Our presence will be oblivious to all who reside there."

"What do you mean?" I asked.

"We cannot be seen, nor can we be heard or detected in any way. You will observe many things in each of the lands. We will move from one place to another almost instantaneously. Perhaps even other planets at times."

"Other planets?" The words escaped my lips before I could stop them.

"Yes, Dr. Ambrose, and please do not become unduly alarmed as you appear to be even now. It is indeed as promised, the journey of a lifetime. In this place, time is their continuum, not ours. What may appear as a year or years in the Lands of Circles, will in actuality only be about ten days for us. Some of the inhabitants of these lands are very similar to us in features, while others are very different in their appearance. Never doubt their intelligence, for you will discover that they are far more intelligent than the both of us."

"What do you mean different?" I asked.

"Different has many meanings Dr. Ambrose. Those with our human-like features are only about one-sixth our size."

"But that would make them only a foot tall." I exclaimed as I continued to do the calculations in my mind.

"Excellent math skills Dr. Ambrose, that is correct, but remember that though some are similar to us, there are many who are very different from us. These differences will not simply be found in the dimension of size. They could be shaped differently, more colorful, or possess abilities that we are not accustomed to. And of course you may see all types of variations in dress and attire. Some will have light emitting circles around their wrists, while others will have them around both their wrists and foreheads. These circles appear only for brief intervals, then disappear and reappear again at certain times."

"Even I myself do not fully understand this phenomenon. Not only are there circles on certain inhabitants of these lands, but the lands themselves are all large concentric circles that get smaller as you move toward the inner-most lands. This is where the genesis of its name originates; The Lands of Circles."

"I appreciate the lesson in the geography of the lands, but I would like to understand more about the circles. Why do they wear them?"

"They are not merely worn Dr. Ambrose. They are actually a part of who and where they are; just as a general's stars represent who he is and where he is relative to rank. Their circles remind them of how important it is to observe the sacred laws of communication by which the Lands of Circles are governed. As they communicate and interact with one another, these laws and rules assure their ascension. However, if these sacred laws of communication are broken, their violation will with all certainty, assure the descent of the violators."

"It is also noteworthy Dr. Ambrose, to fully comprehend that the circles around their wrists tell them where they are location-wise in the Lands of Circles. As they move closer inwardly toward the center circles, which are apparently the most important circles of all, they acquire new circles around their wrists for each new land into which they enter. At least this is what I have been able to observe during my stays here in the Lands of Circles.

If they progress far enough, at some point a circle appears around their foreheads. However, I must admit that I am unaware and ignorant to many of the going-ons here in the Lands of Circles relative to laws of the circles in the different lands. However, I do know that all of the circles are representative of forward movement into new lands."

"What do you mean by the laws of the circle of different lands; and that forward movements are from the outer most circles toward the inner most circles?" I inquired, while there were still many other questions exploding in my mind begging to be asked.

"You will learn this and much more before your journey ends." The gentleman smiled.

"This is unbelievable." I was loudly uttering before I knew it. These repetitive outbursts of mine had now developed into a habit. "Little people with circles on their wrists and foreheads in a place called the Lands of Circles, which is located out in the middle of nowhere."

"It is unbelievable only if you are limited in your thinking Dr. Ambrose. Because your practice is based upon restructuring one's thinking, or cognitive restructuring, then your new schema or basic thought needs to be that nothing is impossible in the Lands of Circles."

"Well how is it that no one has discovered this place before now?" I challenged.

"Open your black bag." The gentleman asked with his finger pointing at the bag that I had held in my hand from the very inception of my journey.

I hesitated initially, but complied beneath the weight of a stare that demanded compliance. "There, it's opened, now what?"

"Take it out and look at it."

I knew that he was talking about the global positioning system that I had prudently thought to bring with me. My thinking was simple. I knew that under the circumstances, I needed every advantage possible. "You couldn't be interested in this old thing?" I contended as I pulled the GPS out of the bag.

"Yes, I am very interested in that old thing." He mockingly responded.

Quickly, I held the GPS system up to my face in an effort to hastily ascertain my location before it could be taken. "It's broken. What did you do to it?" I demanded.

37

"What a ridiculous question for a man of your intellect Dr. Ambrose. I never touched it and besides, if you examine it more closely, you will discover that it works perfectly fine; just not here. We are in a different dimension that could never be identified by such a primitive apparatus as that, because this place. . ." He paused. "It does not exist."

"What do you mean, it does not exist?"

"That is quite simple. This place is only here for the period of time that you are here. When you leave, it leaves." I knew that he detected the palpable look of skepticism that was boldly written all over my face. "In time Dr. Ambrose, in time you too will become a believer, and let me assure you, once it happens, your life will never again be the same. By the way, I am now permitted to answer one of the questions that you asked earlier. My name is Beacon. I'm a sort of guiding light for those who providence has chosen for this journey. Here, try putting these on." He said while extending to me a pair of peculiar and odd looking eyeglasses.

"What are these?" I questioned.

"These, my dear Dr. Ambrose are the glasses of perception."

"What do you mean glasses of perception?" It was a question that my curiosity compelled me to ask. I wanted to know everything; and I wanted to know it now.

"Perception, Dr. Ambrose, is reality. It is how we view the world that we live in. In your dimension, people go through life with glasses of perception on all of the time. Oh they are not literal glasses as these are of course, but none the less they have them on all the time. And what they perceive is their own reality, because perception is reality. You do know that don't you Dr. Ambrose?"

"Yes. Yes I do." I managed to stutter out a Rogerian position on perceptual reality before he interjected.

"Listen closely Dr. Ambrose. Reality is what we perceive it to be; no more and no less. Even the word reality is closely connected to the word relative. So our realities are relative to what we perceive them to be. Now please do not get reality confused with actuality. Actuality means what is absolute and real outside of our own perceptive interpretations."

"So, what is reality to one person can be a different reality for someone else, as in "one man's trash is another man's treasure." However Dr. Ambrose, what is actuality for one man is also actuality for another, such as water boils at 212 degrees Fahrenheit. This will always be the same, given certain atmospheric conditions. It is not subject to experiential referencing or perception. Now back to the instructions on these glasses."

"Never take these glasses off, because if you do you will permanently lose the ability to see this most charming and enchanting place. For without these, no one, not even I can see the Lands of Circles."

As soon as I placed the glasses on my face I noticed that we were no longer standing on the shore. There was now a faint glow coming from Beacon's face. Around his wrists and forehead were thick glowing circles. Before I could ask any questions, in an instant, without another word being spoken, we were transported to the Lands of Circles.

CHAPTER THREE
The First Circle

"Remember," Beacon said. "We can neither be seen nor heard." He held up a map of sort very briefly. I could see the different lands in their concentric circular layout. I could see lines, some thin and others very thick. He quickly rolled the map up and continued with his monologue. "What we will witness will be largely about the art and science of communication and interactions. However, they will be placed in a whole new light. There are many lessons to be learned, so pay special attention to all that you see, hear, feel or sense. Always be aware of the land that we are in and the circles that each person displays on their wrists."

"Why is that so important?" I asked.

"It indicates the level at which they interact and communicate." Beacon answered. Before I could ask the next question, he answered it as though my mind was as transparent as glass. "You may be wondering why some of the lines between the circles are thicker than others or why some of the circles are larger than others. You will discover the answer to these and other questions in time."

41

I now knew that he had allowed me to only momentarily see the map. It was probably more for the purpose of raising my curiosity than to answer my questions. While I was pondering on this fact, without notice, and in less time than it takes to blink an eye, we were transported to an entirely new place. The land was amazingly exotic and sort of scary all at the same time. The journey was like being warped through time and space while passing through brilliant arrays of lights bursting and exploding with vivid colors and sounds. I was extremely frightened and excited all at the same time. It took a great deal of effort to maintain my composure while asking, "Where are we?"

"We are in the land of the first circle. Listen and observe." Beacon whispered. "And remember; never remove your glasses of perception."

I was amazed as I immediately saw two of the little people that Beacon had spoken of walking quickly toward us. Without effort or energy we moved along the side of them as they were passing. We were somehow reduced to their size and moved as if we floated on air. We were like invisible shadows that followed their every step. Their conversation could be clearly heard. They appeared to be searching for something as they rummaged through one bush after the other and looked under one rock and then another.

"Who are they?" I asked.

"The young man is Izzy and the young lady is Lizzy. Let's watch and listen, for there is much to learn and our time is limited."

"Where is the key?" Lizzy asked in frustration.

"If I knew sweetie, would I be looking so hard?" With a furrowed brow of consternation Izzy continued, "Besides, having to lift all of these heavy stones is serious back straining work."

"Yes and searching through all of the shrubbery is aggravating my allergy." Lizzy agreed.

"What are they looking for?" I asked Beacon.

"Izzy and Lizzy are looking for the key. It's not just any key, for you see, only one key will fit."

"Fit what?" I asked. "Can't they just get another key made?"

"It's not that kind of key." Beacon laughed. "They are looking for the answer key. They are trying to get into the land of the first circle of the Special One."

"Who is this Special One?" I asked. "And what's so special about him or her anyway?"

43

"The identity of the Special One is something that you will discover later."

"I found it!" Lizzy screamed. "I found it. I found it."

Izzy rushed to her side. "Great! You've found the key to the first circle of the Special One. Open it up."

"No." Lizzy smiled. "I will give you that pleasure." She said handing the sealed scroll to Izzy.

"Wow." Izzy sighed slowly. "Let's find a place to sit down. My knees are getting weaker by the moment."

"Yeah, so are mine." Lizzy said as they sat together on the trunk of a large fallen tree.

"Here goes." Izzy said as he broke the seal. They both held their breath as they unrolled the scroll to see the following:

THE KEY TO CIRCLE ONE IS RESPECT; KEEP THIS KEY FOR ALL OTHER CIRCLES . . .

"I don't understand this." Izzy declared. There was a short pause before he repeated himself. "I just don't understand it."

"Wait Izzy. Just relax and let's take our time here. I'm sure if we put our heads together we can figure this out. I mean it can't be that difficult." Again they both sat on the large fallen tree searching diligently for the solution to their dilemma; a dilemma that was hidden in the words of the scroll that was now stretched out before them.

"I've got it!" Izzy jumped up and shouted. "Let's go to the great Tree of Wisdom and ask her. Surely she will know." With that said they both began running hand-in-hand up and down and around winding curves through the heavily foliaged trail.

"What is the Tree of Wisdom?" I inquired of Beacon, as I watched them running hurriedly and panting loudly as they made their way through the forest.

"You will see in a moment, for the great Tree of Wisdom is just ahead of them. I will tell you this much, in the entire world there is only one such tree of its kind."

Suddenly Izzy and Lizzy both stopped in front of an enormously large tree that seemed to be aglow with a soft golden radiance that emanated from every side of it. Even the soil around its roots shimmered.

"Tree of Wisdom! Tree of Wisdom!" Lizzy called out. "Mam, we do hate to disturb you, but we need your help in a very important and even urgent matter."

"Izzy and Lizzy, it is good to see you again. You both know that it is my pleasure to answer your questions. After all, you must never forget, that is why I am here." Looking at their wrists and noticing no furry or lighted circles, the great Tree of Wisdom exclaimed, "No circles, so if I am correct, you are about to start a new relationship with someone who is new to the both of you. And may I ask who might that be this time?"

"This time it is with the Special One!" Izzy blurted out excitedly. "We are going to start a relationship with the Special One."

"My, my, the Special One." The great Tree of Wisdom pondered. "So you're going to build a relationship with the Special One. How much do you know about the Special One?" The great Tree of Wisdom asked.

"Very little, in fact nothing at all except that he is a good and decent person." Izzy and Lizzy responded simultaneously.

"Well you need to know more than that." The great Tree of Wisdom laughed. "Pay very close attention to what I have to say. First of all the Special One is really the Special Ones."

"Huh?" Lizzy exhaled noisily in disbelief.

"The Special Ones?" Izzy echoed.

"Yes." The great Tree of Wisdom smiled. "The Special Ones are really an incredibly special couple. But the two are referred to as the Special One because of their very, very special relationship with one another. If you can make it to their inner circles, you will clearly understand why they are called the Special Ones. Well why did you come to me in the first place?" The great Tree of Wisdom asked.

"Oh yes, we almost forgot." Izzy smiled somewhat embarrassed. "Here Lizzy, you read it." He said passing the scroll to her.

"THE KEY TO CIRCLE ONE IS RESPECT; KEEP THIS KEY FOR ALL OTHER CIRCLES . . ." Lizzy read aloud with a puzzling intonation in her voice.

"Oh that is really quite simple." The great Tree of Wisdom offered. "In order to begin a relationship with the Special Ones, the key is to show respect at all time. You must respect each of them and especially respect their relationship with each other. You must also show respect for one another. Do you understand what this means?"

"Yes." Lizzy stated emphatically. It means that we must respect them as individuals and equally important, we must respect their relationship with each other, as well as our own relationship with each other."

"That is it." The great Tree of Wisdom laughed. Now for the second part."

"Second part?" A perplexed Lizzy asked.

"Yes, there is a second part. It says keep this key, for all other circles."

"Oh, I see." Izzy and Lizzy smiled at one another.

"That means that each key will be accumulative. That simply means that though respect is the key to the first circle, it will also be very important in each successive circle."

"But how will we know if we are violating the Special Ones' rule of respect?" Izzy interjected.

"The answer to that is also very simple. If you make it to their first circle, which is called the Circle of Respect, you will notice that the first lighted circle will appear on your wrists. If you violate the principle of respecting the Special Ones, the circles, which will appear occasionally for short-lived periods on your wrists, will disappear and you will be immediately expelled from their Lands of Circles." The Tree of Wisdom continued.

"Expelled?" Izzy questioned, while cringing at the very thought of it.

"Yes. And there is never an exception to this principle by the Special Ones. You see, if the Special Ones allowed anyone to violate this principle, it could destroy even their very own special relationship with one another. You will understand this more clearly as you make your way from one circle to the next. And that is what you must now begin doing. You have enough information to make your way to the first circle of the Special Ones. So on your way." The great Tree of Wisdom laughed. "Now on your way." She continued. Izzy and Lizzy turned and began running, when they suddenly stopped and returned to the Tree of Wisdom.

"But which direction do we travel?" Izzy asked.

"Yeah." Lizzy added, "How do we find our way?"

"The way will find you." The Tree of Wisdom laughed again as Izzy and Lizzy started their journey to the land of the first circle of the Special Ones.

CHAPTER FOUR
Into the First Circle

"Look!" An excited Izzy shouted to Lizzy as he pointed straight ahead. "It actually found us!"

"The Tree of Wisdom was right again." Lizzy shouted in a hush whisper. "The way found us."

They came to an abrupt stop as a wide eyed Izzy and Lizzy stared with opened mouths as they stood at the entrance to the land of the first circle of the Special Ones. A large wooden hand carved sign was posted at the entrance that read, "EVERYONE THAT ENTERS OUR CIRCLES MUST ENTER THROUGH THIS PATH." Without any hesitation the pair dashed quickly pass the sign. All along the pathway were smaller signs reiterating again and again "THE KEY IS RESPECT."

"Wow do you see that." Lizzy asked.

"How could I not? These signs are everywhere." Izzy responded. After a brief pause he continued. "Listen, do you hear that?"

"Hear what?" Lizzy questioned.

"That!" Izzy repeated emphatically. "Listen closely."

After a moment or two, came a declaration of excitement, "I hear it." Lizzy announced with a look of surprise on her face. There were soft whispering voices in the distance. But it was as if they were coming from every direction.

"Respect is the key." The voices proclaimed softly at first and then loudly and softly again.

"We don't have to run to the great Tree of Wisdom for this one." Lizzy smiled.

"Yes." Izzy agreed. "The first circle is the Circle of Respect. It surrounds and permeates all of the Lands of Circles."

"This respect thing must really be important." Lizzy commented in a solemn and sobering tone.

"It must be." Izzy agreed. "I wonder what the consequences are if it is not observed?"

"I don't know." Lizzy whispered, "But I don't think that I want to find out either. After all, the Tree of Wisdom did say something about being immediately expelled from the Lands of Circles."

"MAKE WAY! MAKE WAY! MAKE WAY!" someone was loudly yelling aloud. They were repeating these words with intensity and urgency as the words became louder and louder and the clamor and disturbance seemed to be rushing toward them.

"Move!" Exclaimed an excited Izzy as he took Lizzy's hand and hurried her off of the pathway.

Two people were being hastily and forcibly escorted out of the Lands of Circles of the Special Ones. They were being rushed pass Izzy and Lizzy like a fire truck on its way to a five-alarm fire. "MAKE WAY! MAKE WAY! MAKE WAY!" They continually yelled until they had gone pass them and down the path, across the bridge, and all the way out of the land of the Special Ones.

"I wonder, what was that all about?" Izzy asked Lizzy as they both cautiously stepped back onto the cobblestone pathway.

Before Lizzy could open her mouth with an answer a raspy voice rang out behind them.

"They violated the basic rules of respect."

"Ah!" A startled Izzy and Lizzy cried as they jumped away from the direction of the sound as they turned to face it.

"Who are you?" Izzy asked, while trying to catch his breath as Lizzy eased behind him.

"Where did you come from? You almost scared us to death!" Lizzy exclaimed as she came forward.

"Where did I come from? Where did I come from?" The man asked somewhat confused by the question. "The question is where did the two of you come from and where do you think you're going?"

"I'm Izzy and she's Lizzy, and we're entering the circles of the Special Ones."

"Who told you that you were entering the circles of the Special Ones?" The man was growing taller by the minute. As he grew he was forced to bend lower and lower to enable him to talk face to face with Izzy and Lizzy.

"Well . . ." Izzy began before he was abruptly cut off.

"Humph." The white haired man grunted in a throaty manner as he popped up a few more inches in height. "I am tired of all of the riffraff that we have to throw out of the Lands of Circles of the Special Ones. Do you even know who I am?" The man leaned forward toward Lizzy with his eyes squinted and one side of his mouth curled upward in a distorted sort of snarl.

"No Sir." Lizzy stuttered.

"Who are you sir?" A bold Izzy cautiously asked, while stepping between the man and Lizzy.

"Sir? Did you say sir?"

"Yes sir." Izzy and Lizzy responded simultaneously.

"Umm, maybe you're not riffraff after all. That's very respectful of you. This head full of white hair should stand for something, but I see people all the time who do not know the meaning of the word sir. Nor have they any idea of what true respect is all about. You must respect everything in the Lands of Circles. RESPECT! RESPECT! RESPECT!" He screamed. But as he heard himself he spoke much softer and began shrinking back to his normal size. "Oh I'm sorry. I did not mean to yell." He apologized while rubbing his hand through his white hoary head of hair. "But I was not yelling at you. It's just that I am still so upset."

"Upset about what sir?" Lizzy asked.

"Did you see all of the commotion that just took place? I mean the "MAKE WAY! MAKE WAY! MAKE WAY!" The old man was yelling again. "Oh my goodness." He said as he heard himself. "There I go again, yelling I mean." After a brief pause he stated, "That's my job you know. My name is Mr. Siren. I have to clear the way for the riffraff to be removed from the Lands of Circles as soon as possible."

"Who are riffraffs sir?" Izzy inquired.

"They are those who violate any of the rules in the Lands of Circles of the Special Ones. They are most dangerous you know, my, my, most dangerous. We must rid the lands of them as soon as possible."

"Sir may I ask where are we in the Lands of Circles of the Special Ones?" Izzy smiled nervously.

"My, just look around you. Can't you see that you're in the Land of the Circle of Respect? This is the foundation of all of the other lands. No matter which other land you enter, always, at its foundation, there will be the rudiments of the Land of the Circle of Respect. If you ever fail to respect the Special Ones, regardless of which land you are in, I will be on you in an instant." He snarled. "Oh my, there I go again getting excited. It seems to be becoming an occupational hazard."

"Be on us in an instant?" Izzy replied with his curiosity nearly peaked.

"Yes, in an instant. And just like that couple that was just thrown out, I mean escorted out, you too will have to go. Can you believe it?" The old man asked.

"Believe what?" Lizzy responded.

"They actually almost made it into the Circle of the Land of Friends. That is one of the lands in the inner circles you know. That means that they were on their way to getting pretty close to the Special Ones. Pretty darn close, I tell you. Well we live and we learn and that will not happen again." The old gentleman offered.

"Sir, how does it work? I mean how do we get into the lands of the inner circles?"

"You mean you don't know?"

"Sir we haven't a clue?" Lizzy softly and sadly confessed.

"You appear to be good kids, so listen up and pay close attention to the details." The old gentleman pulled out a large pad with colored markers.

"What you are about to discover is how the different lands are laid out and how to move from one land to another." This is the picture of the lands that the white haired Mr. Siren drew with his colored markers.

"There are eight initial lands in the Lands of Circles. The outer most land is called the Circle of Respect. Notice that it surrounds all of the other lands. Also observe that you cannot enter any other land without first going through the circle of the Land of Respect.

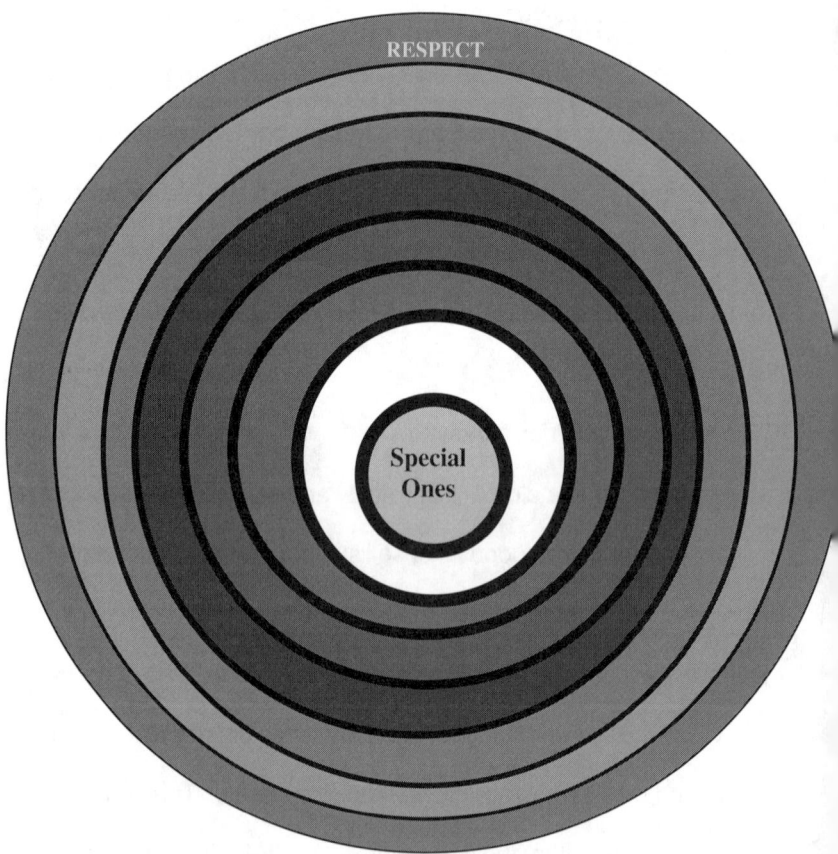

Notice that as you progress to each land in the Lands of Circles, you will become aware of two distinct principles. First of all each circle will get progressively smaller than the circle before it. That is because there will be fewer and fewer people in each land. You will understand the reason for this as you move through each land. Also pay close attention to the line or border that surrounds each circle or land. Do you see that they get thicker and thicker as you move toward the inner circles of the Special Ones?"

"Yes, they do." Izzy and Lizzy answered.

"That is because the thicker lines represent walls that show that it will become more and more difficult to move from one land into the next. Especially remember that it will become very difficult as you move closer inwardly toward the Special Ones. So you have to ask yourself, are you really sure that you want to try and get closer to them." Mr. Siren instructed.

"Yes, we're very sure." Izzy and Lizzy insisted.

"We want to know what it is that makes them so very special." Izzy continued. "You see, Lizzy and I are going to get married soon and we want to have a special relationship like the one that the Special Ones presently share. We believe that if you're going to make a copy of something, the first thing that you have to do is to make sure that the original is worthy of duplication. And from everything that we have researched on the Special Ones, we believe that we can learn a great deal from them. It is not that we want to duplicate them. We believe in our own uniqueness, but we know that we can learn so very much from them."

"Yes." Lizzy added. "We're in love; and it is a special love. However, we want it to be really special, and we've heard that the Special Ones have a very exceptional relationship, and that is our reason for wanting to learn whatever we can from them."

"Very noble," muttered Mr. Siren. "Very noble indeed. If you pay close attention to the rules and follow them, you should have no problems. If you have any questions, just call out to the Info-Bugs."

"How can we help you?" Several little high pitched creatures with wiry voices cried out all at once.

"Oh no." Mr. Siren said, "I was just telling them if they needed to know something, all they had to do was call on the Info-Bugs." Mr. Siren turned to Izzy and Lizzy. "See how they just popped up when I called their name."

"Yes." Lizzy responded. "But what are Info-Bugs?"

"What!?" One of the Info-Bugs responded.

"What are Info-Bugs?" Another chimed in.

With that, a chorus of the Info-Bugs began to sing.

"We are the Info-Bugs. We know almost everything.

Ask us any question, and we'll make the answer plain."

"Enough." Mr. Siren laughed. "You can all go now. And if you hear your name called in the next few minutes, please do not respond. I will be telling Izzy and Lizzy about how wonderful you are." Just as quickly as the furry little Info-Bugs had appeared, they disappeared even more quickly.

"Where did they go?" Izzy asked in astonishment.

"Wow! They left so quickly." Lizzy laughed. "And excuse me for saying it, but they looked so cute and cuddly; real huggable, and funny."

"Yes, they are funny indeed." Mr. Siren laughed. "I love their little furry faces. They're so amusing and short and you almost never see their legs. To be perfectly honest with you, I don't even know if they have legs." They all laughed out loud. "But there is one thing for sure." Mr. Siren offered as the laughter subsided. "They will always tell the truth, one-hundred percent of the time. And when they don't answer you it is because they don't know the answer at that moment, but you can be sure that within a few seconds or minutes they will certainly get the correct answer for you. You see, that is what they do best."

"Is that all they do?" Izzy asked.

"Oh no." Mr. Siren laughed. "They do much more than that. Remember the scroll that said, the key to circle one is respect; keep this key for all other circles."

"Oh yes, it was at the entrance to the Land of the Circle of Respect." Izzy and Lizzy smiled.

"Well that sign, and all the other signs that you have seen or will see were made by the . . ." Mr. Siren looked all around and cupped his hands around his mouth and whispered as softly as he could, "the Info-Bugs. We have to whisper their names or they will show up, if you know what I mean." Mr. Siren, Izzy and Lizzy all laughed together.

When the laughter stopped, Mr. Siren was on his way. He never said a goodbye or even see you later. He simply rushed away while Izzy and Lizzy were caught in the thralls of laughter. "Did you see that?" Lizzy asked Izzy. "No one ever says goodbye around here."

"They are here one moment and gone the next." Izzy agreed. After a brief pause while both Izzy and Lizzy took some time to reflect on all of the comings and goings, Izzy continued. "My, speaking of here one moment and gone the next, it's time for us to be gone also." Izzy and Lizzy hurried away hand-in-hand not quite knowing what was ahead of them.

"Mr. Beacon, how will they make it to the next land?" Dr. Ambrose asked.

"That, you will discover in time." Mr. Beacon said didactically. "Remember Dr. Ambrose that time discloses everything and keeps very few secrets."

"Keep up." Izzy laughed, while holding Lizzy by the hand, as they both ran down the path that they hoped was leading them to the next land.

As they were running, suddenly Lizzy and Izzy were stopped dead in their tracks. "Do you see what I see?" Lizzy asked.

"Yes, there is a circle around our wrists. How did it get there?" Izzy inquired.

"I don't know." Lizzy innocently admitted. "Do you think; could it mean;" she paused and then took a deep breath before finishing her sentence. "Do you think that we have actually made it into the Land of Respect? And could it be that already we are on our way to the borders of other lands? Maybe this circle even shows where we are in our relationship to the Special Ones."

They were both very excited to know that their journey had actually begun and they were so happy to see the proof of their movement forward as indicated by the circles that were now glowing around their wrists.

Izzy paused in the midst of their jubilation. He was suddenly very deep in thought as he slowly articulated, "There is only one way to be sure." Though he was amazed and astonished at the circles on his wrists, he wanted to know their true significance. He could not help but stare at them. They had no weight; none at all. It is as if they were beams or rays of light. Finally, with his breath abated, he took his finger and moved it toward the circle. He was even more astonished when his finger passed right through the circle all the way to his wrist.

"Look Lizzy, it's light. The circles around our wrists are beams of light." It was with a great deal of effort that Izzy could finally turn his eyes away from his wrist and look at Lizzy.

"It is?" Lizzy asked in disbelief as her finger was now piercing the circle of light around her own wrist.

"We should call the Info-Bugs. They will know for sure what this means."

"Info-Bugs at your service." Several of the Info-Bugs shouted after appearing out of thin air.

"How can we help you?" Still others asked as they all hovered in mid air forming a large furry circle around Izzy and Lizzy.

"We would like to know what does this circle of light around our wrists mean." Lizzy smiled nervously.

"Allow me to take this one." One of the Info-Bugs volunteered as he moved forward. "The circle means that you have spent sufficient time in the circle of the Land of Respect, without violating any of the principles of the Special Ones. This means that you are now in a position to move toward the border of the next land in the Lands of Circles."

Instantly, the Info-Bugs all disappeared. "I was right, we are about to move toward the next Lands of Circles." Lizzy smiled with confidence.

"I never doubted you for a moment." Izzy said as the two momentarily embraced.

"We must get underway immediately." Izzy suggested as he turned toward the thick bushes ahead of him. "Maybe it is just beyond these bushes." He asserted as they moved ever forward beaming with excitement and hope.

"There is only one way to find out." Laughed a happy and ecstatic Lizzy, as she closely followed on his heels. They both made their way through row after row of thickly foliaged hedges.

"Stay very close." Izzy laughed and encouraged Lizzy. "I don't want to lose you in here." He laughed again softly as he struggled with the small branches of shrubbery pressing against his face.

"I'm right here." Lizzy assured. "But keep talking just in case. It's getting pretty hard to see."

Finally Izzy and Lizzy made their way into what appeared to be a clearing. There it was; a sign of enormous size. "Welcome to the Land of Acquaintances." Izzy read triumphantly.

"Come on." An enthusiastic Lizzy yelled as she ran ahead of Izzy through the clearing, pass the sign and onto the path to which it pointed. "Look at all of the little signs along this path saying, don't forget respect." Lizzy read one after the other though they all were saying the very same thing. She was exhausted from the long run and so was Izzy. They stopped near a large boulder to catch their breath.

"I bet you that these signs are the work of the Info-Bugs." Izzy said aloud.

"Info-Bugs at your service." Several voices rang out simultaneously. And then one after the other they enthusiastically spoke.

"We can answer almost anything." One of the Info-Bugs shouted.

"And what we don't know we can find out in a flash." Another interjected.

"How do you like our signs?" A third Info-Bug eagerly inquired.

"Don't touch these. They're still wet. You got here sooner than we expected." Another laughed.

"Yeah, we painted these just for you."

"Whoa. Slow down, you're making me dizzy." Izzy chuckled.

"What's so funny?" Lizzy giggled contagiously.

"Get it?" Izzy laughed. "Dizzy Izzy." The Info-Bugs, who were easily prone to laughter, all joined in. It was a hilarious sight. The harder Izzy and Lizzy tried to stop, the more they laughed. Finally the laughter faded from hysterics to a few snickers.

"Well?" Asserted one of the Info-Bugs somewhat urgently.

"Well what?" Izzy replied with his curiosity peaking.

"Why did you call us? We're busy you know."

"Yes, busy, busy, busy." The rest chimed in. Some had low pitched scratchy voices, while others were high pitched and squeaky.

"But we didn't call you." Lizzy offered guardedly.

"Oh but you did. We all heard you." They clamored on one accord.

"Oh you're right." Lizzy said. "Izzy, do you remember when you said, "I bet you that these signs are the work of the Info-Bugs? But we weren't calling you."

"No, we were just admiring your remarkable work. But since you are here, maybe you can answer another question for us." Izzy implored.

"Yay, a question!" They all fervently cheered and clapped.

"What is it?" One of the Info-Bugs asked in a hush voice, as all of the Info-Bugs grew silent. Their eyes and ears literally grew larger right before Izzy and Lizzy's eyes as they anxiously anticipated Izzy's question.

"We've come this far by listening to the Tree of Wisdom. And we even have a circle on each wrist." Izzy whispered, while raising his hands to show off the circles. The Info-Bugs' ears and eyes grew even larger, as all of their little mouths were now shaped like little O's as they nestled closer and closer to Izzy and Lizzy.

"But the question that we have now," Lizzy interjected, "is how do we get into the next land?"

"Do you mean the Land of Acquaintances?" The Info-Bugs added as they all pointed toward a towering wall.

"Yes, look at it." Izzy and Lizzy said. "There is a thick wall all around it. How are we supposed to get in?"

"You will eventually view that little wall as nothing." One of the Info-Bugs differed with Izzy and Lizzy's assessment of their plight. "Keep in mind that as you move from one land to the next and closer to the Special Ones every wall will get much thicker, higher, and much more difficult to cross."

"Yes." Another Info-Bug continued. "But you must be patient, persistent, and above all respectful."

With that said, the Info-Bugs all vanished in a split second. "Wow! They did it again. Do you see how quickly they disappear?" Lizzy asked Izzy somewhat bewildered.

"Amazing, simply amazing." Izzy grinned. "Well let's forge ahead to the Land of Acquaintances."

After hours and hours of trying to find an opening through the wall, Izzy and Lizzy finally stumbled upon a large metal door. It was like no other door they had ever seen anywhere up to now. It was bolted and locked from the inside. "I'm tired." Izzy sighed aloud as he flopped to the ground.

An exhausted Lizzy almost immediately crumbled beside him. "Remember," Lizzy encouraged him as she precisely enunciated each of her words, "we are to be patient, persistent, and above all respectful. We cannot stop. We simply must keep trying. Others have had the strength and belief to make it in and so will we."

"I'm not thinking about quitting sweetie." Izzy responded lovingly and tenderly to Lizzy. "I just need to rest for awhile, just long enough to catch my breath."

It was at that very moment that the pair was startled and shaken by a loud clang and thump that was heard coming from the other side of the door.

WHO'S IN YOUR CIRCLES

CHAPTER FIVE
The Land of Acquaintances

Jumping to their feet Izzy and Lizzy quickly ran back several steps from the oncoming door.

"Watch out!" Izzy shouted as he grabbed Lizzy's hand and pulled her toward him.

They could barely believe their eyes, as the massive metal castle-like door slowly swung open. They found themselves retreating even more to make room as the enormous door rattled, screeched and crackled its way toward them as it opened wider and wider on its huge squeaky hinges.

Without looking behind him, Izzy, quickly backing up just a little more for safety and clearance, suddenly yelled "Ow!" He had bumped his head hard against a large low-hanging tree limb.

"Oh my!" a nervous voice rang out from the other side of the door. "Please tell me that I did not hit you with the door. We are so careful you know. After all, this is all that we do in each of the lands. We open the doors and we close the doors. Now please tell me that I did not hit you with the door."

"No." Izzy replied as he rubbed the back of his throbbing head. "I bumped my head on this tree limb." He said pointing to indict the limb in question with his other hand.

"Good. That is very good. I don't mean bumping your head of course, but it is so good that the door did not hit you. I have been doing this for many years, and my father and uncles did it before me and their fathers before them. It's a family tradition you know; and in all the many years we have never struck anyone with a door. That is why we will not oil the hinges. They make enough noise to warn everyone around to look out because something is happening."

"Excuse me sir, but may I ask who you are?" Lizzy inquired.

"Oh my, I'm so sorry. I did not at all introduce myself did I? Of course I didn't. Or you would not be asking who I am; what was I thinking about? I guess I was distracted by the young man yelling after bumping his head. How egregious, how unconscionable, we Keymen always introduce ourselves upon sight. That's our way you know. And I mean always." He pondered for a moment. "At least we did until now." He nervously laughed.

"Oh you have nothing to be sorry about. Nothing at all sir." Izzy smiled. I'm Izzy and this is my fiancé Lizzy. We are trying to enter into the Land of Acquaintances."

"My name is Mr. Keyman, and it is so nice meeting you both." Mr. Keyman extended his hand which was covered with a bright white nearly glowing cotton glove.

"Please to meet you." Izzy said as he shook Mr. Keyman's gloved hand.

Lizzy soon followed suit, but as she shook his hand she held on and said, "Oh my, I have never felt material so soft or seen anything so white. I'm a seamstress by trade." She added to qualify her statement.

"Yes and she is one of the finest seamstress of all." Izzy interjected with a smile.

Lizzy continued. "And if there is one thing I know it is cloths and fabrics. And in all of my years I have never felt a material so soft or seen one that was so white. I've seen denim, rayon, nylon, silk, gabardine, polyester, cotton of course, linen, even fine linen, wool, hemp, ramie, spandex, natural and synthetic material and ..."

"I think he understands honey." A slightly embarrassed Izzy offered approvingly as he smiled at Lizzy.

Mr. Keyman looked at his hand, which was still being held by Lizzy and cleared his throat as a signal for her to release it.

"Excuse me." Lizzy smiled as her eyes wandered back and forth between Mr. Keyman and Izzy. "No offense intended." She continued as she finally released his hand.

"And none taken." Replied Mr. Keyman. "You're right, this is a very special material; one of a kind you know. It is woven using a very unique process that has been in the family almost forever. But the truth is stranger than fiction in this case. You see, we must have this very special material and only this material for our very special hands. No other material will suffice." Mr. Keyman offered.

"What is so special about the material?" Lizzy questioned.

"Oh, it is more about our hands than the material."

"What is so special about your hands?" Izzy blurted. They look just like Lizzy's and mine except for those unusual and very special looking gloves."

"You must remember that you are not in Kansas anymore." After an awkward pause Mr. Keyman burst into laughter.

"But we're not from Kansas." A puzzled Lizzy replied. "Of course you're not." Mr. Keyman continued to laugh softly. "It's just that I've always wanted to say that." "Why?" Izzy pried.

"Oh, it's not important, another era, another place, another time. However, what I am trying to say to you is that everything is not as it appears to be here; and everything here is not as it appears to be. You must never forget that." Mr. Keyman laughed confidently. "Oh, but we are wasting time. Do come inside." Mr. Keyman said as he led the pair through the gate.

Izzy and Lizzy hurriedly followed and watched closely as Mr. Keyman quickly closed the door. "We close it a lot quicker than we open it." Mr. Keyman laughed nervously as he looked around. "We do not want any riffraff to enter you know."

"Wow!" Lizzy smiled as she lit up with excitement. "Look at our wrists!" She exclaimed to Izzy. They had both successfully achieved their second circle of light.

Their attention was quickly redirected to Mr. Keyman by the sound of the big bolts on the door being thrown, but these were not the only bolts as they would soon discover. "Izzy, you asked why was it that my hands were so special, well now it is time for you to find out." With that said, Mr. Keyman slowly removed the glove from his right hand and then his left. At a snail's pace, he neatly folded each glove and carefully placed them in a pocket inside the large and oversized checkered vest that he wore. "Now observe what happens when I touch each keyhole on the door."

"Oh my!" Izzy slowly breathed in disbelief. "The strangest things, I keep seeing the strangest things." He continued as he stared in amazement. Mr. Keyman's hands were beginning to change and take on a whole new shape. Right before Izzy and Lizzy's widened eyes, his hands turned into hard golden metallic images that were shaped like large skeleton keys. They were bright and shiny like newly polished golden trophies. They matched the large shimmering "F" shaped emblem that hung on a golden chain around his neck.

Before Izzy and Lizzy could respond with words, Mr. Keyman placed his hands into the two large locks and turned one clockwise and the other counter clockwise. Clang-bang, went the two internal door bolts. Afterward, Mr. Keyman slowly withdrew his hands from each lock. He closed his eyes and took a deep measured and slow breath as his hands reassumed their original human-like form.

Mr. Keyman immediately placed the gloves very methodically onto his hands. "We must throw both the internal and external bolts on all doors. Of course they can never be opened by anyone, other than a Keyman."

"Thank you for allowing us to enter." Lizzy offered politely.

"It was not my doing." Mr. Keyman asserted. "It was the decision of the Special Ones. They are the only ones who can allow entrance through each and every door."

"But how do they know us?" Izzy added.

"That's just it; they don't really know you yet." Mr. Keyman smiled. "That is why you have been allowed only into the Land of Acquaintances. The Special Ones have been carefully observing you since you both first entered into the Land of Respect. They have watched how courteously you dealt with others, and they commissioned me to open the door for your entrance into the Land of Acquaintances."

Izzy and Lizzy turned to each other and recited together, "Be patient, persistent, and above all respectful."

Izzy turned to Mr. Keyman and asked, "Would it be respectful to ask what does the F represent on the chain around your neck?"

"Sure it would be respectful. There's nothing secretive or magical about it. All of the Keymen must wear them. All of our letters represent the initial to our first name. I am Fredd, with two dees, Fredd Keyman. Should you be fortunate enough to make it through each gate into new lands, you will always be greeted first by another Keyman. They are all my brothers or first cousins. There is Edd, Tedd, Jedd, Nedd and Redd; and we all have two dees at the end of our names of course."

"Oh yes." He continued. "And the answer to your question young lady about the whiteness of the glove is the cloworms. They are like silk worms filled with white and colorful lights. The material they weave for our gloves can only be done when they are filled with their whitest of white lights; blinding white!" He emphasized. "And these very special cloworms are indigenous only to the Lands of Circles."

Again Izzy and Lizzy looked at each other for just a moment and when they turned to talk with Mr. Keyman, he was gone. "How do they do that?" A frustrated Izzy asked.

"I don't know." Lizzy laughed. "But did you hear what he said? The Special Ones are watching us."

"My, my," Izzy sighed. "He did say that didn't he, didn't he? My, my, my."

"I would like to have some of those special little cloworms for myself." Lizzy laughed out loudly. "I would make something amazing for us to wear on that special day when we are privileged to meet the Special Ones."

In the middle of their private and personal conversation they suddenly became aware of voices. When they looked around they could not reason among themselves as to where all of the voices were coming from. They were voices engaged in various conversations about any and everything.

Suddenly, the Land of Acquaintances was filled with a multitude of people, all engaged conversationally as if they were there all along. "Who are all of these people?" Izzy asked.

"How did they just appear? I mean where did they come from?" Lizzy added.

"I know; let's call on the Info-Bugs." Lizzy smiled with excitement.

Before Izzy could object to Lizzy's suggestion. "Info-Bugs to the rescue." A chorus of the little fuzzy creatures, all of various colors and sizes rang out.

"How can we help?" One asked.

"We're very helpful you know." Another boasted.

"Yes, helpful indeed, helpful indeed." A third Info-Bug laughed.

"Who are all of these people?" Lizzy questioned.

"They are all of the people that the Special Ones are acquainted or getting acquainted with, like yourselves." One Info-Bug replied. "You're in the Land of Acquaintances." He continued.

"But it's a little more involved than that." Another Info-Bug added. "They are all of the people that the Special Ones are aware of, and who the Special Ones see as respecting themselves, each other, and of course the Special Ones also."

"And that is why you are here." The first Info-Bug hovered in closely while smiling in Izzy and Lizzy's faces. "You respected the Special Ones enough to want to know more about them, and you have honored all of their rules that you have been made aware of at this time."

"You must prepare to be here for awhile." Another Info-Bug injected.

"To be here awhile?" Lizzy questioned.

"Yes, you must observe everyone closely before you allow them near or your life will be filled with regrets." A little blue Info-Bug soberly whispered.

"This is where you will be very closely observed to see if you will learn, understand and demonstrate respect for each and every rule of the Land of Acquaintances."

"Rules? What rules are we to learn?" Lizzy asked.

"Most of them are on the sign over there." The Info-Bugs exclaimed as they pointed and stared toward a large sign nestled among the branches of surrounding trees.

"Thanks." Izzy and Lizzy yelled. And without saying another word or hesitation they hurriedly made their way toward the sign. In their excitement and anxiousness to see what was written on the sign, they never noticed that the ever-helpful and extremely informative Info-Bugs had made their usual unannounced departure. Nor did they notice that the many people who were standing around and conversing had vanished, and their surroundings had completely changed. They only noticed the sign in the distance toward which they were now propelling themselves as fast as their legs could carry them.

They were not being selfish in ignoring everything and everyone around them. They were not being disrespectful to the Info-Bugs with only a cursory thank you. They were simply focused in their desire and hope to gain greater insight into the minds of the Special Ones.

"Made it!" Izzy exclaimed as they came to an abrupt halt in front of the sign. Together they both earnestly began reading and absorbing the very precious and valued information that was written there.

RULES FOR THE SPECIAL ONES AND FOR THOSE ENTERING INTO THE LAND OF ACQUAINTANCES

1. Everyone must respect the Special Ones and one another at all times.
2. Those in this land are the guests of the Special Ones.
3. The Special Ones must communicate only on an acquaintance level in this land.
4. Everyone who occupies this land must communicate in an environment of love, honesty, trust and respect.
5. The Special Ones must keep people in the Land of Acquaintances long enough to thoroughly observe them.
6. The Special Ones alone are in control of who stays in this land.
7. The Special Ones have not only the right, but an enormous duty to keep all people out of the Land of Acquaintances who would dare to violate its rules. If these sorts have entered this land and afterward violate its rules, the Special Ones are obligated, by virtue of the potential threat to their relationship, to put them out immediately upon discovery of such violations.
8. The Special Ones must seek to be on one accord in regards to who is allowed in and who is to remain outside of this land.
9. The Special Ones must not allow their feelings alone to control their decisions. Their decisions must be based on what they observe relative to their own personal experiences.
10.   There is no substitute for time investment and a thorough examination of all of those allowed into this land.
11.   No one must go beyond this land unless they meet all criteria.
12.   When disrespected the Special Ones must immediately expel those committing such acts outside of the most distant circles.

"Are these written for us?" Lizzy asked.

"I don't think so." Izzy answered. I believe that they are written for the Special Ones. Even though rule number one says that everyone must respect the Special Ones at all times. It is not talking directly to us, but to the Special Ones.

"Oh I get it." Lizzy agreed. "When we see that everyone is to respect the Special Ones at all times, then we are to understand that this rule is telling the Special Ones not to allow anyone to disrespect them or the very special relationship that they enjoy with one another. So the rules are to protect the Special Ones and their very special relationship. Our part is to know the expectations of the Special Ones so that we do not violate any of their rules."

"You've got it!" Izzy smiled. They stood there in front of the sign for quite awhile. They read it over and over again. They discussed the meaning of each rule and the implications that they each had on how they were to govern themselves in the lands of the Special Ones.

"Well what do you think?" Asked a curious and now well-read Lizzy.

"I think that we better be very careful to follow each of them." Izzy responded. "And besides, they are really the same rules that I would want for you and me."

"Yeah, my thoughts exactly." Lizzy smiled. "I want our marriage to be strong like the Special Ones."

"It will be." Izzy vowed.

After what was six months in the Land of Acquaintances Izzy and Lizzy were beginning to wonder if they would ever find their way to the next land, which they had discovered was the Land of Associates. "Lizzy do you think we will ever make it to the next land?" Asked a concerned Izzy.

"Remember the words of the Info-Bugs." Lizzy stated with enthusiasm. "Be patient, persistent, and above all respectful. These are the same qualities that will strengthen our already special relationship." They both laughed and repeated the phrase together. When their laughter subsided just a little, they were startled to see that there were Info-Bugs all around them laughing as well.

"Where did you guys come from?" Izzy asked, while still laughing. He could not help but to laugh. Some of the little furry Info-Bugs for the first time had uncurled.

"Wow you're not little furry balls after all." Lizzy uttered in amazement. She was in awe to see that their little furry under bellies glowed like fire flies. Even more amazing was how their little bellies fluttered vibrantly with bright alternating colors that were like living rainbows. Some had little furry beards; while others were just about bald. In fact, their heads were the only thing that did not have fur. Each one of them were unique and beautiful in various and funny sorts of ways. No two were identical; yet they all seemed the same.

"What did you call us for this time? We're ready you know." One of the bearded Info-Bug smiled with a large broad set of human like teeth.

"Wow!" A wide-eyed Lizzy smiled back. "You have a beautiful set of teeth." With that said, all of the Info-Bugs began to laugh out loud. "What's so funny?" A bewildered Lizzy asked.

"My teeth." The Info-Bug sadly answered. "You see only one in a thousand Info-Bugs have teeth. The rest of them think that it's," he paused. "Well" he said after another momentary pause, "that it's sort of weird. That is why I try not to smile so much." He ended sheepishly.

Lizzy questioned in an encouraging tone to every Info-Bug within the sound of her voice; "You would not laugh at him because he is different, would you?" There was no anger or annoyance in her voice, only compassion for the Info-Bug she believed to be spoken ill of.

All of the Info-Bug simultaneously whispered, "No."

"Of course you wouldn't." Lizzy smiled.

"Of course we wouldn't." The Info-Bugs smiled back at her reflecting her own compassionate tone and facial expression.

"I mean, you talk about respectfulness and being respectful in all ways, surely you wouldn't violate that rule; would you?" Izzy asked.

"No." The Info-Bugs shouted echoing Izzy's sentiments. "We would not violate that rule."

"I know why you all laugh." Lizzy smiled.

"You do?" The Info-Bugs asked in unison as their little eyes grew large in anticipation of her response.

"Well of course I do." And with that said, Lizzy began softly singing this song.

"You laugh because you love him so.

And you're just trying to let him know,

That in your heart deep-down beneath

You adore and love his gorgeous teeth."

The Info-Bugs all responded in perfect accord, while joyfully singing along with Lizzy.

"We laugh because we love him so.

And we're just trying to let him know,

That in our heart deep-down beneath

We adore and love his gorgeous teeth."

They all were laughing and singing when suddenly there was a loud clanging and banging sound interrupting their merry celebration. This was no ordinary clanging and banging that they heard; no, this was an earsplitting sound from behind Izzy and Lizzy that would bring even more joy to them than either could have anticipated.

CHAPTER SIX
A Whole New Land

It was one of the Keymen turning the huge locks from the other side of a huge door that appeared from nowhere. The loud squeaking noise was announcing that the door was opening.

"Come through immediately." Mr. Keyman cried urgently, as Izzy and Lizzy ran toward him. He began pulling the door close. Izzy and Lizzy made it through the closing door just as it slammed closed behind them.

Mr. Keyman was laughing as he extracted his large metallic like hands from the locks in the large castle like door. He closed his eyes and took a deep breath and his hand reassumed their humanlike form. After a brief pause he removed a pair of glowing white gloves from his inner vest pocket and ceremoniously placed them on his hands and resumed laughing.

"What's so funny?" Izzy questioned emotionally.

"The two of you are." Mr. Keyman continued to laugh. "By the expression on your face, I can tell that the Info-Bugs really pulled one over on you. It is the only deception allowed in any of the Lands of Circles."

91

"Huh?" Izzy responded, while scratching his head.

"What do you mean pulled one over on us and deception allowed?" Lizzy asked still not seeing the humor that gave Mr. Keyman the impetus for his laughter.

"Oh." Mr. Keyman continued in a somewhat softer tone of joviality. "Did the Info-Bug with the big toothy smile get picked on by the other Info-Bugs?"

"Yes, we were very concerned for him." Lizzy whispered.

"It was all only a ruse." Mr. Keyman began his boisterous laughter again.

"What do you mean all only a ruse?" Izzy Inquired.

"You know, a hoax, a trick, a stunt." Suddenly Mr. Keyman possessed a very serious tone as he leaned in closely to Izzy and Lizzy. "The Info-Bugs would never disrespect one another. The purpose of their trickery was to raise a response from you."

"Huh?" Izzy and Lizzy mumbled.

"Don't you see?" Mr. Keyman continued in a very serious tone as he leaned even closer to their faces. "It was your being irritated and your intolerance of their taunting of the toothy Info-Bug that was the very thing that caused the Special Ones to cue me to open the door for you. Don't you see? It was all a test; a very necessary test. Look at your wrists!" Mr. Keyman directed.

Izzy and Lizzy could not believe their eyes. There on each wrist were now three circles where there were only two before. "We made it!" Izzy and Lizzy shouted jubilantly as they hugged one another while excitedly jumping up and down.

"Listen." Mr. Keyman interjected interrupting their celebration.

Izzy and Lizzy tried to calm themselves as they both turned toward Mr. Keyman to do just as he requested and listen to him. It was then that they both noticed the large shiny E hanging from his neck. "You must be Mr. Edd Keyman." Izzy smiled.

"Almost, more precisely the name is Mr. Eddward Keyman, with two dees."

"My apologies sir, no disrespect intended, it's just that . . ."

"None taken young man. I am sure that Fredderick informed you that my name was Edd, with two dees. However, that was only out of habit. You see, in our nucleus family, we all addressed each other by our informal first names, because that is how our parents addressed us as we were growing up. Oh but enough with our personal family history, please excuse me sir and madam, and allow me to formally

93

greet and welcome the both of you." With his voice mimicking that of an announcer of a three ring circus, he began to exclaim, "Mr. Izzy and Ms. Lizzy, on behalf of the Special Ones, I embrace the privilege of inviting you both to the Land of Associates."

"The Land of Associates?" Izzy and Lizzy repeated in sweet disbelief and excitement.

"Oh, but thank you sir." Lizzy smiled broadly.

"And that goes for me too sir." Izzy broadly grinned.

"In the scheme of things, not many people make it to this land. This is truly a rare privilege that the both of you are presently experiencing. In this land you will actually get to meet the Special Ones if all goes well."

"What?!" Lizzy panted excitedly. "You mean that we are actually going to meet the Special Ones?"

"If all goes well." Eddward repeated.

"Here in this land?" Izzy added. "When? I mean how soon?"

"Of course that depends upon your behavior and the desires of the Special Ones." Mr. Keyman answered. You cannot and will not know exactly when, but you will indeed meet them if you are faithful to the rules and all goes well." He emphasized.

"Will we know who they are?" Izzy questioned.

"You most certainly will." Mr. Keyman laughed softly.

There was a sudden and loud cry, "MAKE WAY! MAKE WAY! MAKE WAY!" Izzy and Lizzy had heard that sound before, so they quickly dashed out of the pathway that led to the gate.

"MAKE WAY! MAKE WAY! MAKE WAY!" Mr. Siren screamed as he ushered out several people from the Land of Associates, all the way out, even beyond the Land of Respect.

When Izzy and Lizzy looked around, Mr. Keyman had vanished. "The strangest things." Lizzy sighed in a barely perceptible undertone.

"Yes, yes." Izzy added. "Strange indeed, strange indeed." It was just then that Lizzy noticed a sign in the distance. It was surrounded by Info-Bugs hard at work. They were busy doing something to the sign, but Izzy and Lizzy were too far away to know what it was.

"Let's go and see what is going on." Izzy said to Lizzy, who had already begun making her way to the sign. "Hey wait for me!" Izzy called out as Lizzy ran ahead of him laughing.

By the time they had both reached the sign, all of the Info-Bugs had finished whatever they were doing and had vanished. Izzy and Lizzy slowly closed in and began staring at the sign together. They spoke not a word as each began silently reading to themselves.

RULES FOR THE SPECIAL ONES AND FOR THOSE ENTERING INTO THE LAND OF ASSOCIATES

REMEMBER RULES ONE THROUGH TWELVE

13. These individuals have gone through two levels of screening already, but you must intensify your scrutiny at this level.
14. If anyone disrespects either of you, they are disrespecting the both of you, for the two are one.
15. You must meet those in this land because you want to meet them and not because they want to meet you.
16. You must meet them when you want to meet them and not when they want to meet you.
17. Do not get too close to people on this level, no matter how genuine and good they are or appear to be.
18. Keep all conversations on an associate level only.
19. Ask yourself why you are allowing those you meet to stay at this level or why are you considering moving them to a closer level.
20. Do not allow the possessions, celebrity status, title, position or outward appearance of those on this level to influence your decision for allowing them to stay here or move closer to your inner circles.
21. Use your experience and base your decisions on that, but also remember that there is wisdom in the counsel of those that you respect for their good judgment demonstrated in the past.
22. Pay more attention to what you see and sense rather than what you hear.
23. Ask yourself, will the development of this relationship move me closer to my desired goals or away from them?

This time Izzy and Lizzy took even more time than they had on the other sign. They sat in a comfortable clearing on plush green grass beneath beautiful willow trees. The surrounding Magnolia-like trees, with large leathery leaves and enormous white blossoms, gave off the sweetest fragrance. There were speedy and colorful humming birds darting between the branches of nearby Formosa trees extracting copious amounts of nectar from their large pink flowers. "Listen." Lizzy softly whispered to Izzy. "Listen to all of the birds."

"I'm ahead of you." Izzy smiled. "Their amazing songs arrested my attention a long time ago." Izzy and Lizzy stayed there for a very long time trying to commit these very special rules of the Special Ones to memory. They lingered there listening and relaxing amidst sweet fragrances and the beautiful music of the many birds that had come to life warbling their inspiring and comforting songs.

"This is truly a beautiful place." Izzy thought to himself as he worked on committing the rules to memory.

"I think I've finally got them memorized." Izzy smiled with a sense of satisfaction.

"So have I." Lizzy responded. "But we have to be sure that we are not only committing the words and sentences to memory, but the true meaning and purpose of each."

"You're absolutely correct." Agreed Izzy as they both sat and relaxed on the plush green grass. Their minds rushed forward as they began to contemplate the deeper purposes and meanings of the Special Ones' rules.

After a good bit of time had passed, they both tenderly looked at each other and smiled approvingly. Their journey into this amazing land had quickly slipped into months. Their journey through the Land of Associates had been very circumspect. They had many conversations with a number of the people who were also traversing there in search of the Special Ones.

Many told of their encounters with the Special Ones in such amazing manners and with such a descriptive passion that Izzy and Lizzy ached and burned with an even more intense desire to meet them. Some of those who had met them, by their own accounts, stated that they had encountered the Special Ones as many as thirty times.

However, even those with the many encounters were still in the Land of Associates. Izzy thought, if he and Lizzy had not met the Special Ones even once, then how could they even possibly hope to move forward any time soon. Talking about moving forward, the truth is that Izzy and Lizzy did not even have an idea as to when or even if they would meet the Special Ones for the first time any time in the near future.

Some of the couples that they met had given the following advice to Izzy and Lizzy; that if moving on was their only goal, then they would soon be ushered out of the lands in a compelling and quick fashion. "Relationship should be your goal." Several of the associates of the Special Ones had advised. Izzy and Lizzy took the advice to heart and expressed their gratitude.

On this day Izzy had planned a special outdoor lunch as a surprise for Lizzy. It was to take place soon. He had done everything within his power to keep it a secret. Though big within his heart, the day arrived with no more fanfare than the day before. "Come and take a walk with me." Izzy grinned as he took Lizzy by the hand, giving it a soft and much welcomed caress.

"Oh Izzy!" Lizzy laughed as she entered the clearing and stared at the area prepared by Izzy. "When did you get the time to plan this and how did you get everything up here?"

"Don't be concerned about the details sweetie. I'll tell you later, but right now I just want you to enjoy this very special moment prepared and intended for the most precious jewel in all of creation."

"And who might that be?" Lizzy coyly teased.

"Um, let me see." Izzy played along as he scratched his head.

With that spoken, Lizzy held Izzy closely and kissed him softly on his cheek. "I'm the happiest girl in the whole world!" She whispered into his ear.

Izzy hugged her around her waist and picked her up and began spinning in a circle and shouted louder and louder, "I love you Lizzy and I'm the happiest man in the whole universe." Izzy tumbled onto the ground laughing and exhausted. Lizzy then sat beside him and they both made their way onto the blanket that Izzy had carefully spread over the thick green grass. They laughed, smiled, and gently held each other as they enjoyed their food, their surroundings, and especially one another.

"Hi." A couple of voices rang out immediately drawing their attention toward them. A beautiful young couple that appeared to be several years older stood above them gazing down with approving smiles.

Izzy and Lizzy quickly stood to their feet and extended their hands. "Hi." Izzy said. "I'm Izzy and this is my fiancé Lizzy."

"Please to meet you." The young man said. "I'm Bill and this is my wife Jill."

"Please join us." Lizzy invited.

"We have plenty of food and we would love your company." Izzy added. Bill and Jill accepted their invitation and sat down to converse and dine with Izzy and Lizzy. They were talking and laughing and really enjoying one another's company when Lizzy noticed it. She awkwardly tapped Izzy on the leg while pointing at Bill's and Jill's wrists. Izzy almost choked on his food as he immediately comprehended what Lizzy was communicating to him.

"Please excuse my pointing." Lizzy offered. "I certainly do not mean to offend you in any way. But everyone else that we have seen in this land had only three circles around their wrist just as we have."

"But the two of you have seven." Izzy stuttered in wonderment.

Izzy and Lizzy both gazed into each others eyes as if they were communicating telepathically. They then turned and looked at the seven circles around Bill and Jill's wrists and immediately jumped to their feet. They could barely get out the words that they somehow spoke in concert. "The Special Ones, oh you must be the Special Ones." Izzy and Lizzy were continuing to walk backwards without even noticing what they were doing.

"It's alright." Jill smiled. "You are correct. We are many times referred to and known as the Special Ones."

"Please." Bill said as he and Jill took several steps forward to catch Izzy and Lizzy by their hands to keep them from backing farther away. "It's really alright." Bill continued. "We get that response all the time, but we are mortal, flesh and bones just like you."

"But you're the Special Ones." Lizzy blurted.

"Yes, but what makes us special is our relationship with one another. It is more than just our knowledge of the rules that enhances and strengthens our relationship. It is truly understanding and valuing the importance of implementing them in our lives as we continue to nurture and develop our relationship with one another and those in our inner circles."

"We will visit you at another time." Bill said. "It will give you time to absorb all of this." In a moment, before they could blink their eyes, Bill and Jill were gone. Izzy and Lizzy were alone and more confused now than ever before. It was simply incredible. They had finally met the Special Ones, but now they were left with more questions than answers.

"Where did they go?" Izzy asked.

"Away." Lizzy laughed nervously. Just like everyone else around here, they just vanished. I love this place!" Lizzy laughed out loud. "Wow! We met the Special Ones and they really were special, weren't they Izzy?" She asked.

"Yes they were." Izzy answered. "They were even more special than I had ever imagined them to be. I wonder when will they come around again." Izzy hesitated. "They said they would visit us at another time."

"I declare." Lizzy asserted. "That is exactly what they said isn't it? But you and I both know that their return visit will be predicated upon our conforming to the rules not just by the letter, but even more with sincerity on adhering to the intent of the rules."

"Make no mistake." Izzy interjected. "The rules are still extremely important, but something tells me that establishing rapport and developing a genuine relationship with the Special Ones is equally as important."

"That means being ourselves." Lizzy stated.

"Yeah, we truly have to be ourselves, because that means being honest. I was just thinking, that maybe, perhaps." Izzy paused as he reflected on what he was about to say.

"What were you thinking Izzy?" Lizzy inquired.

"Well," Izzy continued. "I think that it's time to call, the you know who. What about you? What do you think?"

"The you know who?" Lizzy asked somewhat confused.

"Yes, the you know who." Izzy smiled.

Then the epiphany came. "Oh, the you know who." Lizzy smiled. "Let's do it."

"Info-Bugs." They both called out.

"Info-Bugs are at your service." A big blue furry Info-Bug spouted. There were an army of them, all waiting to fulfill Izzy and Lizzy's requests.

"I guess that you know that we have finally met the Special Ones. If I am not mistaken, you have been around them for awhile right?" Lizzy asked.

"Been around them forever." One of the Info-Bugs laughed.

"Been longer than that." Another group of the Info-Bugs laughed even louder.

"Let's just suppose for the sake of supposing." Lizzy smiled awkwardly. If you could come up with an A-1 formula for communicating with the Special Ones, what would it be? I mean just supposing."

"A-1?" one of the Info-Bugs echoed Lizzy's words.

"Yeah, we all heard her. She said A-1." Another Info-Bug commented with a raspy, but little childlike voice.

All of the Info-Bugs that were present huddled into a literal big circular three dimensional ball. They began to levitate, hum and glow in different, but uniform colors all at the same time. Neither Izzy nor Lizzy had ever witnessed this behavior before. "The strangest things." Izzy whispered softly. "The strangest things."

"Yeah." Lizzy smiled in agreement as she stared.

Instantly the Info-Bugs blew apart like a child's soap bubbles on a breezy summer day. They were all nodding their little round heads in agreement. "We believe that the A-1 formula for communicating with the Special Ones must be similar to the formula that they use for communicating with one another." A little red Info-Bug with more fur on the top than bottom, asserted firmly.

"Love would be the first quality." Another suggested.

"Honesty would be the second." Said another.

"Do not forget Trust." Another Info-Bug yelled from a distance.

"And please children, always remember respect." An older and more mature looking Info-Bug wisely counseled Izzy and Lizzy.

"Let's put it on a sign." One of the Info-Bugs with a small paint bucket and brush smiled. Instantly, standing before Izzy and Lizzy was this sign:

**IT IS DIFFICULT TO HAVE
TRUE COMMUNICATION IN A
RELATIONSHIP WITHOUT:**

1. **LOVE**
2. **TRUST**
3. **HONESTY**
4. **RESPECT**

Izzy quickly turned toward Lizzy and asked, "That's exactly how we communicate ourselves isn't it Lizzy?"

"Sure it is." Lizzy smiled. "I think that is why the Special Ones are so special to us, because we have so much in common." She beamed.

Lizzy looked around for the Info-Bugs who were now long gone. "They did it again." Lizzy laughed. Everyone comes and goes so quickly here." She continued.

"Have you noticed also how fast the days seem to come and go?" Izzy inquired of Lizzy.

"Yes, my, my, time really does seem to fly in this place." Lizzy agreed.

And time really did pass through the Lands of Circles like little squalls of wind rushing from their unknown origins to far away destinations. And just like the little leaves that were swept away in the flutters of swirling winds, Izzy and Lizzy rode the eddy currents of their good fortune and wise decisions to happier and more blissful times than they had ever experienced before. They were enjoying the ride, even though they were still uncertain of their exact destination.

Again, the sun stole a gentle kiss from the sky to create a most beautiful morning. Izzy and Lizzy took notice of its golden beauty and in unison broke into broad and glowing smiles. They had been so diligent in their determination to enjoy their lives in the Land of Associates. They clearly understood the importance of their desire to enter a more intimate relationship with the Special Ones.

The advice of the strangers in the Land of Associates had found a receptive place in their hearts and left an indelible imprint in their minds. They had now determined that they would fully enjoy wherever they were in the lands, and extract the most pleasure possible from each moment of their journey. This morning was no different in that regard. But their bodies could not endure the desires of their hearts. If possible they would have spent the entire day moving about. But the reality that they had to reluctantly embrace was that they were very tired. They slowly made their way through another line of trees only to be confronted by a rapidly flowing river. What they did not know was that the river encircled the entire land that lie ahead of them.

"Wow!" Izzy exclaimed. "What a beautiful river."

"Look at the water." Izzy continued. "Look at how clear it is."

"There's a sign." Lizzy announced as she pointed over Izzy's shoulder. They both ran the short distance and were extremely exhausted as they deeply and rapidly breathed, almost gasping for air as they peered at the sign. It was written with regular alphabets, but they were all jumbled.

"Should we call you-know-who?" Lizzy asked with a puzzled look on her face as she sat down to catch her breath.

"I don't know." Izzy responded. "I think that we should try and figure this one out ourselves after we have rested for a moment." He added as he sat beside Lizzy. "What do you think?"

"I agree with you one-hundred percent." Lizzy smiled broadly. "We can do it. After all, we both know that we won't always have the you-know-who in our lives." With that said, Izzy and Lizzy, after catching their breath, pensively stared at the sign for an extensive amount of time. This is what they saw.

> **abc defcd hi**
>
> **jcacdkelmaehl**

Izzy and Lizzy returned to the sign for many days trying to figure it out, when one day only a few steps away, Lizzy noticed a piece of painted wood mostly obscured by nearby vines. Attempting to pick it up, they had to wrestle it from the clinging tendrils of the vines that wrestled for its possession. Lizzy noticed this code: a=t; b=h; c=e; d=r; e=i; f=v; h=o; i=f; j=d; k=m; l=n; m=a. "Izzy!" She shouted excitedly. "Look at this."

"It's what we've been looking for and didn't know it." Izzy could barely contain himself as he was suddenly flooded with excitement. He gazed upon the letters. They were the same letters that were on the sign. After a few moments came a shout of victory.

"I've got it!" Izzy declared loudly. "The sign says, The River of Determination."

"That makes plenty of sense." Lizzy agreed. "Entering this next land requires determination and commitment."

They both then turned their attention and marveled at the crystal clear River of Determination that flowed pass so swiftly. The reflection of the rays of sunlight caused it to sparkle like highly polished shimmering white diamonds.

Still amazed, Lizzy gasped "It's so deep and clear."

"Yes and wide too." Izzy added. "How will we ever get to the other side?" He questioned apprehensively.

"Like the name says, with determination." Lizzy laughed. Izzy knew that Lizzy was the spark plug in the engine of their relationship. "Good old positive Lizzy," he thought, "encouraging me just when I need inspiration." They both broadly smiled in agreement as their hearts gave birth to new born levels of resolve, determination and conviction.

It was thirty days later. The river was still crystal clear. It still flowed rapidly. It seemed even wider, and the sunlight still sparkled on it like shimmering white diamonds. Izzy and Lizzy were still having difficulties in their efforts to cross it.

"We've tried everything, but we have not moved one inch farther in over thirty days." Lizzy stated in frustration.

"I know." Izzy replied softly while smiling to encourage his encourager. "Remember the very special rule that we've learned earlier; be patient, persistent, and above all respectful."

"I know." Lizzy agreed with her lips slowly curling into a smile. They both became more determined and committed to work not just harder, but smarter.

"Remember what they say." Izzy shouted happily. "If at first you don't succeed, try and try again."

"That's good, but I have a different one." Lizzy laughed. "If at first you don't succeed, think and try again." They both laughed as they repeated. "Think and try again."

One day, after quite a few months in the Land of Associates and several very special meetings with the Special Ones, bang, bang, bang came a series of loud and explosive thumps against Lizzy's cottage door. It was at a time when Izzy was visiting Lizzy for an evening meal. The two cottages to which they were assigned had always been next door to one another in each of the two preceding lands of circles. They had become very comfortable with this type of arrangement and hoped that it would not change anytime during their stay in the Lands of Circles.

"Hurry!" It was a voice coming from the other side of the door.

Izzy ran to open the door and was surprised to see that no one was there.

"Who is it?" Lizzy asked as she sprang from her chair and ran to Izzy's side.

"I don't know." Said a confused Izzy as he scratched his head and looked around. "But it's not an "is" any longer. It's more like a "was." But I could have sworn that I heard someone yelling for me to hurry."

"You did." Lizzy assured him. "I heard it too." Izzy and Lizzy walked a few paces from side to side and all the way around the outside of both their cottages, but they saw no one; not a single soul. This was very perplexing.

"Well let's go back inside. Izzy tried to be humorous. "Maybe it was a large talking woodpecker."

"Woodpeckers don't talk." Lizzy laughed nervously.

"Yeah, but are you forgetting where we are?" Izzy sighed deeply while laughing to comfort himself. "The strangest things happen here, the strangest things."

"Look Izzy!" A shocked Lizzy called out while pointing toward the door of her cottage. "It's a sign."

"So that is what was going on. They weren't knocking. They were hammering a sign onto the door."

"But I heard them say hurry." Lizzy challenged.

"Yeah, but it could be that they were talking to each other and saying hurry up and finish putting up the sign." Izzy reasoned.

Izzy and Lizzy read the following sign that was attached to the front door of Lizzy's cottage.

> *You are invited to a grand dinner in the Land of Friends at the request of the Special Ones. The time is 7:00 PM tonight. Your transportation will arrive at 6:30 PM.*

"Look Izzy!" An excited Lizzy called out while pointing at Izzy's cottage door. "The same sign is also on the door of your cottage."

Six-thirty came quickly. Izzy and Lizzy could not believe their eyes. A beautiful rose colored carriage drawn by what appeared to be four large and very furry Info-Bugs arrived. Neither Izzy nor Lizzy had ever seen Info-Bugs even a tenth of their size. "It's right on time." Izzy said as he looked at his watch.

"The coach is absolutely stunning." Lizzy smiled, stared, and sighed all at the same time. Izzy escorted Lizzy through the open door of the carriage that was being held open by the driver.

After the door was closed with Izzy and Lizzy sitting securely inside, the coach never appeared to move. It is as if they were instantaneously transported to the front of a huge iron gate without really moving. The gate had a boldly embossed metal sign attached that read "The Land of Friends." The now familiar sounds of the large bolts being thrown by one of the Keymen were like welcoming music to their ears. Sounds that had once frightened them now brought them comfort. As the rustic old gate slowly swung open they could see one of the Keymen with his large metallic hands and the medallion around his neck gleaming in the twilight.

As the carriage unhurriedly moved forward and passed the Keyman, he closed and bolted the gate. After momentarily closing his eyes, and slowly exhaling, his hands again resumed their human-like form. He quickly put on the glowing white gloves to cover them and immediately turned toward the paused carriage and greeted Izzy and Lizzy with a very warm smile.

"Welcome to the Land of Friends where travelers are few and the journey rare." His voice was deep like still waters, but with a clarity that resonated throughout the carriage. Suddenly the inside of the carriage lit up with an amazing burst of light. It was a luminous event that concluded as quickly as it had begun.

"Did someone flash a camera?" Izzy asked in awe.

"I don't think so." Lizzy Replied.

"Look at your wrists." The deep voice of the coachman burst forth with laughter. "You have just entered the seldom traveled, but marvelously warm Land of Friends!" He exclaimed. There were beautiful glowing new circles on each wrist.

"Oh my!" Lizzy shrieked. "We're friends with the Special Ones. How can that be when we've had so little interaction with them?"

"Quite the contrary." The coachman declared as he dismounted the halted coach to interface with Izzy and Lizzy. "Everyone that you have interacted with in your extensive stays in each of the lands, were in fact directly connected to the Special Ones. And may I humbly add that this declaration even includes me? You see, put quite simply, you have been interacting with the Special Ones and they have been interacting with you."

"Do you remember the story of Cinderella and how the prince interacted with her without ever knowing who she was until the glass slipper was placed on her foot? And of course you have heard of the story of the frog who was really a prince. And there was the millionaire who carried himself like a peasant so that he could gauge people's true feelings about him. Then there was the Prince and the Pauper."

"You know that it has even been said that some have entertained angels unaware. All through life we encounter people who are not what they appear to be. However, in the case of the Special Ones, they are everything they appear to be and much more. It is just that they often choose to be who they are through the ears, eyes and hearts of each of the permanent residents of the Lands of Circles. Don't you get it? As you do unto us, you do unto the Special Ones."

"Wow! How do they do that?" Lizzy whispered.

After pausing for a moment the coachman leaning in toward Lizzy whispered even more softly, "Just like you, I don't know either." Then he became louder as he leaned backward, "I don't have a clue." Then even more loudly, "And I don't even want to know." With that said, the coachman began to heartily laugh out loud. For a brief moment Izzy and Lizzy were filled with consternation, but they both gave in to the laughter of the coachman and assumed his carefree outlook. They themselves, though nervously at first, eventually exploded with unfettered laughter.

When the laughter subsided, "You really have come a long way." The coachman smiled while emphasizing the word "long."

Lizzy turned to Izzy, "We really have." She softly breathed the words into his ear.

"Yes dear." Izzy smiled as he gently held her in his arms. "We have made it a very long way."

"Indeed you have." The coachman replied again with laughter. "You have even made it beyond the River of Determination."

With that said the coachman reestablished his position atop the carriage and did a most unexpected thing. His laughter was interrupted by song. He happily sang in the tune of a light hearted Irish jig. As the words flowed from his lips, the coach began to gracefully flow through welcoming streams of air that flowed gently over Izzy and Lizzy's faces.

"Do you hear that?" Lizzy asked Izzy. "The coachman is singing, and I think he is saying our names." The coachman was singing a most delightful song, but he was not at all singing alone. Izzy and Lizzy heard hundreds of voices.

"Izzy and Lizzy deserves a hand.
They've made it to a brand new land.
With the Special Ones they are now friends.
In a place where few have made it in."

Izzy and Lizzy stared in amazement out of the coach's open windows. Though they saw no one, there truly were hundreds of voices repeatedly singing these four verses of consolation. All the voices sang in perfect harmony. The baritones, tenors, altos, bass and sopranos all blended for a perfect production of this melodic ode to Izzy and Lizzy. Once again they stared out of the window to look for what they could only hear. It was the Info-Bugs. Hundreds, maybe thousands of them had joined in, but the Info-Bugs themselves could not be seen by Izzy and Lizzy for they had all changed their furs to the color of night. However, what could be seen was spectacular. There underbellies were all aglow, and the sky was brilliantly filled with an array of flashing colors. Izzy and Lizzy eased back into the soft velvet seats of the carriage and looked into each others smiling eyes. They enjoyed the song and the light show until the coach silently came to rest in front of the home of the Special Ones.

When the carriage stopped, so did the song. "Thank you." They both said to the coachman as he quickly stepped down and opened the door of the coach.

"This land is different from every other land." The coachman said. "You will understand this when night has removed her clandestine veil of secrecy. There are new and wonderful things and happenings here. Open your minds." He said as he climbed back into the top seat of the coach. "Open your minds to the wonderful privileges, advantages, and possibilities that friendship brings, but be mindful also of its awesome responsibility."

These were the last words heard from the deep resonating voice of the coachman by Izzy and Lizzy as the coach once again seemed to be carried away by the wind through the tranquil air of the night toward the starry canopy of the heavens.

"Did you see that?" Izzy asked with his eyes straining with excitement.

"He said new and wonderful things." Lizzy added in a somewhat raised voice that reflected her astonishment at what she had just witnessed.

As they began making their way down the cobblestone walkway to the Special Ones' cottage, there was a buzzing around them that caused them to freeze in their tracks. Their heads and eyes moved from side to side as they turned a full 360 degrees to try and discover the source of the sound.

"Looking for us?" A voice asked from a yet to be identified source.

"Info-Bugs?" Lizzy responded. "It must be the Info-Bugs playing a little trick."

"You called?" The Info-Bugs asked appearing all around the confused couple.

"We heard buzzing and thought that it was you." Izzy stated.

"But if it's not you, then who or what could it be?" Lizzy asked even more confused now than before.

"It could be bees." One Info-Bug asserted. "But don't worry, because the bees in these lands have no stingers. They only pollinate the flowers."

"He's just joshing and having fun." Another Info-Bug interjected, referring to the first Info-Bug's answer. The truth is simple. What you have been hearing are the Q-Bugs."

"Q-Bugs?" Lizzy responded, saying the phrase ever so slowly.

"Yes, Q-Bugs. They have been around you from the moment you entered the Land of Friends. If you hear them buzzing it's because they are about to appear to you."

"That is if you don't frighten them off." Another Info-Bug offered.

"Frighten them off, how can we do that and why would they want to reveal themselves to us anyway." Izzy asked.

"You frighten them off by not listening. The Q-Bugs reveal themselves in order to bring quotes of wisdom from what we call the outside world. That is what the Q stands for, quoting."

"Yes and the reason that someone willfully ignoring their quotes of wisdom frightens them, is because they believe that only fools shun wisdom; and they are frightened of only one thing."

"And that is a fool." Another Info-Bug asserted.

"Fools are dangerous because ignorance is their crown and folly is their scepter."

"Hey." A high-pitched, gruffly voiced Info-Bug trumpeted. "His name is Brilliant Burt. We all have names you know. Burt coined that phrase himself."

Another Info-Bug interrupted with laughter. "Pretty soon the Q-Bugs will be quoting Burt." Several more of the Info-Bugs joined in with hearty laughter as Brilliant Burt suddenly looked like Bashful Burt by the expression that was pasted on his face.

"Well, we'll be sure to listen to the Q-Bugs, and we certainly welcome their wisdom." Lizzy said softly.

In a flash, the Info-Bugs disappeared and the buzzing again immediately surrounded them. This time Izzy and Lizzy stood silently waiting for the Q-Bugs to appear.

"Hear a word of wisdom." One Q-Bug trumpeted. There were presently two of them buzzing about Izzy and Lizzy. They were the oddest looking sort that Izzy and Lizzy had thus far seen. They had large wrinkled foreheads. The hair on their heads was long and as white as sheep's wool. There was a radiance or glow around each strand of their hair which appeared as curly rays of light, which seemed perfectly groomed. Their skin was pale, but exceptionally smooth, which caused their large wrinkled foreheads to stand out with even more prominence. They were more head than body, with their eyes as small as peas.

"The word of wisdom is this." The second Q-Bug began with the first joining in. "Friendship is a single soul dwelling in two bodies,

Aristotle." The noise of even higher pitched buzzing signaled their departure.

"Isn't that what we are?" Lizzy asked Izzy as they made their way down the cobblestone walkway.

"It is just like that Aristotle fellow knew us personally." Lizzy replied as they walked hand-in-hand toward the door of the Special Ones. Without any prompting except that of the warm feelings in their hearts, they both began singing the coachman's song under their breath until they knocked on the door of the Special Ones.

"Izzy and Lizzy deserves a hand.

They've made it to a brand new land.

With the Special Ones they are now friends.

In a place where few have made it in."

WHO'S IN YOUR CIRCLES

CHAPTER SEVEN

LESSONS FROM THE SPECIAL ONES

"Come in." Bill said extending a warm invitation to Izzy and Lizzy. "Jill will join us momentarily." After taking their seats, Izzy and Lizzy were soon engaged in a very interesting conversation with Bill.

"Do you have room for a foursome?" Jill asked smiling as she entered the room. Both Bill and Izzy stood to their feet immediately as Jill sat to the table, while Bill slid her chair under her. Jill had what appeared to be four books in her hands.

"If you don't mind my saying so," Izzy began. "Lizzy and I really want the both of you to know that we count it a real privilege being invited into your home, and we do not take this occasion or privilege for granted."

"Yes." Lizzy added. "This whole event is truly special. And we don't know exactly why you have been so gracious to us, but we are happy and excited about the possibilities."

"You are not here by accident or because of chance." Bill responded. Every movement toward us has come as a result of what we have observed in Izzy and you. You could not have known, but there was no way for you to make it over the River of Determination. It is very important that you both know that. In fact, it is also called the River of Termination, because that is as far as most individuals or couples make it. The lesson to be learned at the River of Determination is very simple, no one should ever be able to enter your Circle of Friendship simply because they want to; no matter how determined they are. They should only enter it because you want them there. Do you understand the significance of what we are telling you?"

"I really do." Lizzy shook her head to the affirmative.

"So do I." Izzy followed.

"Great." Bill smiled. "Now give your attention to Jill."

As Jill slowly slid the books toward the center of the table, Lizzy could not control herself. She felt compelled to say what she was thinking. "May I make a statement?" She implored. After no one objected she began, "I am very curious about the books that Jill has. Something tells me that they are very special. However, there is this question that keeps plugging away at my mind that I've wanted to ask, that is if you don't mind."

"Not at all." Jill smiled broadly, which caused both Izzy and Lizzy to be just a bit more comfortable.

"Well it's really not a question; it's more of a comment. When we first heard of the Special Ones, we expected some godlike figures. And after meeting you for the first time, we were mesmerized by your genuine, honest and unpretentious ways. I guess what I'm really trying to say is, every time we meet you we discover more and more just how special you are. And we are learning so much about ourselves in the process."

"May I finish?" Izzy interjected as he pleaded with his eyes to Lizzy.

"Sure." Lizzy responded feeling thankful for Izzy's assistance.

"Lizzy has honestly represented how we feel about the both of you. Yet it seems that what we have discovered most clearly is this. What make you so special are not your possessions, these lands, or even your friends. You see, what makes you so special to us is the unique and wonderful bond of love and respect that exists between the two of you. And that bond is what we believe that we have and are so desperately striving to make stronger in our own personal relationship. We do not intend to make you uncomfortable with flattery or ingratiating types of recitations, but we talk so much about the two of you between ourselves that I knew exactly what Lizzy was trying to tell you."

After an awkward pause, Bill and Jill expressed their gratitude for the kind words spoken by Izzy and Lizzy. "I feel that it is very important that we revisit the lesson that we just taught. Let me repeat, that the lesson taught, though it is very simple, it bears repeating again and again. So listen very closely, no one should ever be able to enter your Circle of Friendship simply because they want to, no matter how determined they are. They should only enter it because you want them there. And you should only want them there if they will enhance your relationship and you can mutually enhance theirs. Do you understand the significance of what we are telling you?"

"Yes." Replied an even more attentive Izzy and Lizzy.

"Now for the reason for which we have invited you here." Jill began as she passed the books to Bill, Izzy, and Lizzy. "Bill and I are in agreement that it is time to share with you some of the more special jewels that have kept and that continue to keep our marriage and our relationship very intimate and very strong. Remember, that there are rules in each land, but this is our personal rule book. Though it is true that all of the rules are important, these are some of the treasured rules that have served us best."

"We have written them down so that when the time presents itself, we are able to share these unique and empowering lessons with our friends." After the word friends, there was a slight pause as they all smiled and briefly looked at one another.

"So let's turn to page one and begin, but remember that these rules are not necessarily listed in their order of importance." Jill continued.

Rule number one: The importance of good communication between an intimate couple or friends cannot be overly emphasized.

"Let me explain this first rule." Bill stressed. "One day I saw this very interesting demonstration. The presenter stated clearly that we all communicate with one another at some level. He then called three volunteers from the audience. He gave one a butter knife, to another he gave a flat tip screwdriver and to the third he gave a power screwdriver with a Phillip tip. He had a single piece of wood. It was a six-foot long 2x4 inch board lying flat on a table with three Phillip-head screws partially screwed into pre-drilled holes that were in the board.

He then asked all three participants to begin screwing the screws into the board at his command. Each volunteer was to try and out perform the other two volunteers. When the competition began, the electric screwdriver with the Phillip tip won hands down."

"The presenter then stated that we all communicate at some level, but here's the kicker. He went on to say that some of us communicate at the butter knife level, while others communicate at the flat-tip manual screwdriver level, and still others communicate at the power screwdriver level. Afterward he went on to emphasize that just like the electric screwdriver, communication is a tool and that we should all strive to communicate at the electric screwdriver level until we can come up with something better. In other words, we should attempt to communicate as efficiently as possible."

"We must not only have the right tools for proper communication, but the proper knowledge of how to use them as efficiently and effectively as possible." Jill interjected. "The initial question that we must all ask ourselves, and give an honest answer to is this, at what level are we communicating with one another?"

"You see," Bill piggybacked on Jill's statements, "How well we function as a couple or as friends is predicated upon our ability to communicate with each other effectively. We have to understand that communication is not only a very important tool, but a tool with specific functions. Used properly it can nurture, build and maintain a healthy relationship. Used improperly, there is no positive functional or meaningful relationship."

"I never thought of it like that before." Izzy smiled.

"Neither had I." Added Lizzy as Jill began with rule number two.

"Rule number two: Know the circles of communication and communicate within the boundary of each circle in the appropriate manner."

"What do you mean appropriate manner? And what are the circles of communication?" Izzy probed deeper.

"Well." Bill began, "That's a great place to start. Let me begin with the Circles of Communication and relationships. There are at least eight circles or levels that we move through on the way to a deeper and more profound awareness of our intimate self. Be very mindful that there are many other circles, but these are the ones that deal with proper communication and relationships. These circles begin with the outer most circle and move toward the inner most circle. They are named after each of the Lands of Circles. They are:

1. The Circle of Respect

2. The Circle of Acquaintances

3. The Circle of Associates

4. The Circle of Friends

5. The Circle of Close Friends

6. The Circle of Intimates

7. The Circle of Intimate-Intimates

8. The Circle of Intimate-self

And the "appropriate manner" means that we must communicate with each person at the level that we have placed them on or allowed them to reach in our circles. For instance, an acquaintance should be communicated with only at the acquaintance level, and an associate only at the associate level and so forth. There is one exception to these rules that we will discuss later." Bill concluded as he detected a look of confusion on Izzy's face.

"I still don't quite understand." Izzy replied.

"Maybe I can shed some light on this subject." Jill leaned in and began to explain. "Bill is saying; when you communicate to someone, stay in your proper lanes of traffic or in this case your proper circles. Do not cross communicate from one circle to another. In essence do not switch lanes improperly. Communicate with an associate only as an associate. Do not communicate with an associate as a friend, or an acquaintance as an associate. When you cross-communicate in this manner you begin to build malcommunication bridges across the different levels that will almost always lead to uncertainty and confusion."

"I got it!" Izzy laughed softly. "I really think that I understand what you guys are saying."

"Yes, it makes so much sense." Lizzy joined in. "But I must admit that we have broken this rule quite a few times in the past."

"That is so true." An almost stuttering Izzy sheepishly confessed.

"I will tell you like my grandmother told me." Bill joked. "When you know better, you do better. At least that is the belief that we live by." Bill and Jill together acknowledged.

They all turned the pages in their books to reveal the next rule as Jill began reading it aloud.

"Rule number three: What you say with me stays with me."

"Can you clarify that a little Jill?" Lizzy asked.

"I'll be happy to do so and Bill you can jump in anytime you're ready." Jill continued, "Let's say that Bill is speaking to me on a friend's level. I then go and share that information with someone else. Bill finds out about it in a roundabout way. He knows that I was the only one that he shared that particular information with. How do you think Bill will feel when he discovers this?"

"Betrayed!" Lizzy exclaimed. "And he would have every right to have those feelings wouldn't you agree?" Lizzy put the question out to everyone.

"Certainly." Jill answered. "Bill and I follow this rule strictly. No matter what we talk about with each other, what we say to each other stays with us. Here is how it works. Bill and I have a simple rule to help us maintain the integrity of this simple statement of what you say with me stays with me. We simply make the assumption that everything that we say to each other is private. This may seem difficult on the surface, but with a little practice it is really quite easy."

"I see!" Izzy responded excitedly while smiling broadly. "By doing that you don't have to tell each other not to share this or that, because you both already know that whatever you say is at all times confidential."

"Exactly." Bill smiled at the excited Izzy, who was now laughing.

"Now that's special." Lizzy said joining Izzy in laughter.

"This takes us to rule number four." Bill stressed as he turned the page.

"Rule number four." Izzy chorused with high expectations.

"Rule number four: The way you communicate with others will strongly affect how you communicate as a couple or friends." Seeing the puzzled look on Lizzy's face prompted Jill to make additional comments.

"For instance, in our previous example you said that Bill would feel betrayed if he found that I had been sharing information about him with others, is that correct?"

"Yes." Lizzy said.

"Now if I were sharing personal information that Bill shared with me with others, do you think that Bill would continue to share with me?"

"I guess not." Lizzy sighed. "Except maybe he will only communicate with you on a shallow and superficial level." She continued.

"And then your communication with each other will become dysfunctional miscommunication or malcommunication." Izzy interjected.

"That is exactly what happens." Bill concurred. "And as communication goes, listen to this very carefully." Bill leaned forward and continued with a soft intensity. "So goes the relationship."

"Continuous malcommunication of any kind will bring about a dysfunctional relationship. A dysfunctional relationship of any kind will then cause continuous stress. Stress causes diseases and diseases lead to sickness and death. So answer this, who wants to be in a stressful, dysfunctional, and deadly relationship?" Jill inquired.

"These relationships are poisonous or toxic and they will eventually drain all of the life out of you." Bill interjected. "Now who wants to spend their lives being poisoned and drained of their life forces?"

The question was understood by all to be rhetorical. Ergo they just sat there, each answering for themselves and to themselves with the obvious response.

After the pause, Bill chose a different path to explain the detriment and unhealthiness of such a relationship. "Dr. Hans Seyle is considered the father of Stress Management. As a medical doctor and researcher, he won notable awards and recognition for his research on stress and diseases. As an endocrinologist he understood well the relationship between stress and diseases. In short, he said that stress is at the basis of all diseases. So not only is a chronic stressful relationship bad for you mentally, which is obvious, but it is also physically destructive. It literally weakens your immune system and makes you vulnerable to diseases." Chronic stress uses the same hormonal mediators that normally defend the body to suppress immune function (McEwen, 2005). "I do not have to tell you that suppressing the immune system is grave."

"Listen to this." Bill stressed. "Dr. Alfred Coodley states that "Stress is the most widespread medical problem in America today. It's a major contributing factor in 100 percent of diseases" (*National*

Enquirer Conquering Stress, 1985). "One hundred percent; can you believe that?"

"He closed the book in front of him while stating, "Jill and I have prepared a special meal for you guys. We can review more of the book on your next visit, but for now let's just ease up and enjoy the rest of the evening. And never forget that each day is a miracle, with its blessings, opportunities and challenges."

The two couples enjoyed themselves immensely for the rest of the evening. They laughed and ate, and then they ate and laughed, but amid all of their laughter, frolicking and joy, they did not break any of the rules of communication.

As Izzy and Lizzy stood in front of Lizzy's cottage, Izzy held her hands as they watched the carriage serenely zoom heavenward. They were encapsulated in various stages of euphoria as they reflected and reminisced about the joys and wonders they experienced at the home of Bill and Jill.

"Did you hear what Bill said about each day being a miracle?"

"There you go reading my thoughts again." Lizzy expressed with a childlike smile. "I was just thinking how nice it would be to get up bright and early in the morning and witness the birth of that miracle for ourselves."

"It's a date." Izzy confirmed. "We'll meet in the front of your cottage about a half an hour before sunrise."

"What time is that?" Lizzy asked.

"I honestly don't know." Izzy responded.

"The Info-Bugs would know." Lizzy suggested.

"Did someone call the Info-Bugs?" A small red Info-Bug inquired as the rest popped on the scene like popcorn in a microwave oven.

"Of course they did." A sunny-yellow Info-Bug interjected with a smile and a smirk as he popped into view. "That's why we're here. How can we help?" He quizzed.

"We're trying to find out what time the sun rises in the morning, and I'm just curious." Lizzy declared. "What time zone are we in?"

"First thing first." The red Info-Bug smiled. The sun rises at 6:00 AM."

"Second thing second." The other Info-Bug laughed. We're in the Lands of Circles time zone. There's no Eastern, Mountain, Central, Western, Prime Meridian, International or any other type of time zone here. There is only one time zone and that is the Lands of Circles time zone or LOC as we like to call it here."

"We can wake you up you know." The red Info-Bug offered.

"You can?" Izzy asked with an obvious tone of surprise ringing in his voice.

"Of course we can." The other Info-Bug laughed. "We can bang on your doors with our hammers. We build all the signs around here and we do it without a sound. Our hammers make no noise unless we want them to."

"You mean you wouldn't mind getting up that early?" Lizzy questioned.

"Getting up? Oh we don't sleep. We don't need it. We don't get tired and we don't age. We don't get sick and we're always full of energy. What time should we awaken you?"

"You don't get sleepy?" Lizzy inquired.

"What time do you want us to wake you up?" Both Info-Bugs insisted.

"You don't get tired?" Izzy questioned in disbelief.

"What time do you want us to wake you up?" The host of Info-Bugs insisted.

"You don't get sick at all?" Both Izzy and Lizzy tried to find out.

"What time do you want us to wake you up?" Came the unified voices of all of the Info-Bugs that were present.

"5:00 AM for me." Lizzy answered wearily, finally responding to their question.

"5:15 AM for me, LOC time." Izzy added after a pause.

The laughter of the Info-Bugs seemed to reverberate for a moment and could be heard when they could no longer be seen. Izzy and Lizzy each entered their own cottages and their own rooms with warm feelings of anticipation as to what the sunrise would bring at the beginning of a brand new day in the Lands of Circles.

As Izzy faded quietly into his own world of sleepiness, "Imagine that." He thought. "No sleeping, no tiredness, no aging, and no sickness. I read about a place like that somewhere before. My, my, my, what an amazing revelation."

WHO'S IN YOUR CIRCLES

CHAPTER EIGHT
FURTHER LESSONS FROM THE SPECIAL ONES
(Remember the Butterfly)

The banging of the Info-Bugs startled Lizzy as she cried out, "Thank you, I'm awake."

Fifteen minutes later it was Izzy's turn to cry out to the Info-Bugs. "I'm up. Thank you."

As Izzy and Lizzy stepped through their doors, the sun was only minutes from its climb over the ridge of the majestic mountains. They sat there hand-in-hand in hushed anticipation with childlike eagerness. Meanwhile they were listening to the fading nocturnal sounds of nature. When the sun in her brilliance and glory ascended and conquered the towering and massive peaks of the eastern mountain ridge; it was grandly greeted.

There were colorful birds wobbling masterpieces in song that split, pierced, and blessed the cool crisp morning air with unadulterated expressions of life. Boisterous and boastful roosters could be heard in far distance valleys cockling and crowing with bravado as they anxiously strained to be heard.

This spectacular event that they had so often slumbered through without notice or awareness was now being viewed in a whole new light. It was poetry, song, art, love and ecstasy, all coming together in a beautiful and glorious presentation of expression.

Izzy tried to comment on its beauty, but quickly understood that with all of the adjectives combined, there was no language capable of capturing or expressing what his eyes were witnessing. However, he did make a brief effort. "It's incredibly exhilarating, exciting and so invigorating, astonishing and even stimulating. It is miraculously amazing! That is what it is." Izzy proclaimed.

Indeed it was all of that and then so much more. It was the rising of the morning sun. It was at that very moment that a large and colorful butterfly entered this beautiful picture of nature, gingerly landing on Lizzy's inviting shoulder. They were both mesmerized and exhilarated at the splendor of the sight. They were as giddy as little nursery school children at play. The butterfly opportunistically grabbed hold of the gentle breeze blowing under its wings and slowly rose on its currents and silently floated away.

"Izzy have you ever thought about the metamorphosis of the caterpillar into a butterfly?" Lizzy questioned.

"Not really." Izzy responded. "Why do you ask?"

"Oh, I don't know, but I often think about, who told the butterfly that it could fly?"

"Huh?" Izzy giggled curiously.

"I mean, if you think about it, it spent its entire life as a caterpillar inching its way through the dirt, grass, and plants chewing on vegetation. Then one day something inside of it told it to spin a cocoon from which it emerged as a butterfly with wings. Think about that for a moment. Who told the caterpillar that because it had wings it could now fly? Listen Izzy, it had never done anything but inch its way through life, its whole life up to that point. Who told it that it could fly?"

"I guess that it just knows it. Maybe it's something inside of it that nature placed there that spoke to it and said you can fly." Izzy responded.

"I think a lot of people are like butterflies, but they do not hear the voice within that tells them that they can fly." Lizzy stated.

"Maybe, that's our job." Izzy affirmed. "Maybe we are the messengers that are to run to and fro, up and down through the earth and tell people that they are no longer caterpillars and that they can fly." Izzy responded with sincerity.

"I believe that this is especially true as to how we are to conduct ourselves with those inside of our circles. From now on, when we see someone discouraged in our circles, we will say remember the butterfly." They both walked and bathed in the morning's sun singing their newly penned song which they entitled, "Remember the Butterfly."

Again they paused and turned toward the eastern horizon. They silently stood there in the moment and drank in its beauty. They basked in the warmth of its ambiance. They smiled until their faces hurt, but spoke not a single word. Izzy and Lizzy were the willing prisoners of the splendors of nature. They were captive and breathless with their hands locked tightly together. Finally, their overwrought eyes had sumptuously feasted on all that the new day had to offer in its opening scene. The only word for it was "satisfied." Their every expectation had been exceeded. As they prepared to go inside for breakfast, suddenly they could hear it again. It was a buzzing sound.

"The Q-Bugs." Izzy and Lizzy uttered together.

"Are we welcomed?" The Q-Bugs asked seeking permission to speak with Izzy and Lizzy.

"Of course you are, anytime. We need all of the wisdom we can get." Izzy responded with a grin.

"Anytime?" One of the Q-Bugs asked.

"Sure." Lizzy said with a genuine smile.

"Then we don't have to ask for permission in the future?" The other Q-Bug inquired.

"No, not at all." Both Izzy and Lizzy answered.

"Excellent! Then now we begin with words of wisdom from the world beyond our circles."

The other Q-Bug then introduced a new quote. *"This is a day that I have never seen before and will never see again. May I be the recipient and benefactor of its peace, love, hope and joy?* James Harper, Baldwin County, Georgia."

"As you journey through the Land of Friends remember, *One loyal friend is worth ten thousand relatives,* Euripides, Greek playwright."

"What you have said is so true." Izzy said as the stately and wise Q-Bugs vanished before their eyes. He quickly turned toward

Lizzy and continued. "We have never seen this day and we will never see it again. So let's fill it with life."

"Yes." Lizzy responded. "With life that comes without regrets; let's embrace this day and each new opportunity that it brings." She added.

Izzy and Lizzy had a very busy time of it enjoying the new and wonderful things of this joyously joyful day of discovery. They also came up with questions that they desired to ask Bill and Jill. They looked forward to their next evening with the Special Ones, knowing in their hearts that the time shared with them had added rich new dimensions to their already very special relationship.

"Let's go for a walk." Izzy asked Lizzy as he led the way.

"Are we going anywhere in particular?" Lizzy asked.

"No, nowhere in particular, but somewhere very special." Izzy responded.

"And just where is nowhere in particular, but somewhere very special?" Lizzy smiled. It was a line that she had heard Izzy say many times before, but she could never tire of it, because she knew that it was always from his heart.

"Lizzy you know the answer, but please allow me to say it again. The place never has to be any place in particular, but as long as you are there it is always a place that is very special." Izzy smiled broadly. They joined hands and journeyed down a fairly familiar path. "Look up there do you see what I see?" Izzy questioned as he pointed to a sign.

"I see a large owl, but look at it Izzy, it has only one big eye in the middle of its head." Lizzy continued peering upward as she pointed toward its direction, not noticing the sign that Izzy pointed to.

"Wow, I see it too." Izzy said temporarily forgetting about the sign himself, "A one-eyed owl; can you imagine that. It is certainly unique and unique for certain. However that is not quite what I was talking about. It is amazing though isn't it?" Izzy says now lingering on the uniqueness of the one eyed owl.

"Yes, but it seems to have such a sad look on its face." Lizzy commented in a somewhat perplexed tone.

"Yes it does; it appears to be very sad. I don't know, but maybe it's like that because it has only one large eye." Izzy reasoned as sincerely as he could.

"I'm going to call the Info-Bugs on this one." Lizzy said.

"Info-Bugs at your service." Came the familiar greeting. "What can we do for you?"

"We were just curious about the one-eyed owl up in the tree over there." Lizzy directed their attention to the owl by pointing.

"Oh him." One of the Info-Bugs commented.

"He's really quite a story in his own right." Another Info-Bug added.

"He is the only one-eyed owl anywhere. Did you know that?" A third Info-Bugs sadly questioned. "But it's not all bad." He continued. "They say that he has a special and extraordinary talent."

"Yes, he is prophetic." A host of Info-Bugs declared.

"Some believe that he can see into the future." Another added.

"They say, that's the very reason that he is so sad." Still another Info-Bug interjected.

"We've heard that he has only smiled once in his entire existence. No one knows what he saw on that day, but it was recorded, reported, and duly noted that he had a real broad smile on that day." The Info-Bug with teeth added, while demonstrating with his own broad smile.

"This was reported by credible witnesses mind you." Another Info-Bug boasted."

"Do you know anything else about him?" Izzy asked.

"No that's about it." All of the Info-Bugs chimed simultaneously without missing a beat. "He's just a big old one-eyed sad owl. He's the only thing in all of the Lands of Circles that is sad."

"Poor big old sad one-eyed owl." One of the Info-Bugs said just before the owl flew away and the Info-Bugs all disappeared.

After regrouping his thoughts, "I wasn't talking about the owl." Izzy began again conversing with Lizzy. "I was talking about the sign."

"Oh I see, there is a sign, but it wasn't there yesterday." Whispered a surprised Lizzy.

"That's what I'm talking about." Izzy replied as they quickly ran toward the sign. Coming to a sudden stop in front of it they slowly eased forward; leaning to the point of almost falling in their effort to read the following:

> **TO IZZY AND LIZZY, A SPECIAL APPOINTMENT TONIGHT, AT**
> **7:00 PM WITH THE SPECIAL ONES.**
> **YOUR COACH WILL ARRIVE AT 6:30 PM**

WHO'S IN YOUR CIRCLES

CHAPTER NINE
Lessons on the Circles

Izzy and Lizzy were once again sitting at Bill and Jill's table after a wonderful and magical journey on the flying carriage. Their books were now open to where they had left off on their last visit. Jill began this session by saying, "Bill and I have been instructing you from our personal book that is crammed with lessons and guidelines that are very special to us, but what we want to know tonight is do you have any questions of us before we begin this evening."

"Yes." Lizzy responded almost immediately. She was excited to have the opportunity to express what was on her heart.

"What is your question Lizzy?" Jill smiled approvingly.

"Izzy and I noticed that each land so far has had fewer and fewer people. The Land of Acquaintances had many, the Land of Associates had fewer, and the Land of Friends thus far has had very few indeed. Izzy and I discussed the possible reasons for this, but we wanted to see if our way of thinking was correct."

Bill began explaining. "This is not only a good question, but the answer to it is important. The reason the Land of Acquaintances had so many people is because, there are people that you are acquainted with that may or may not be acquainted with you. For instance, I am acquainted with some famous people, who are not acquainted with me. An acquaintance by definition is an individual that one might be familiar with, but who is not particularly an associate or friend."

"So there are many people with whom we have had the pleasure of making their acquaintances, maybe at a social function, a show, church or even in the work place. However, even though we are acquainted with them, we do not associate with them with any meaningful purpose of their becoming our associates."

"Lizzy have you ever been to a social gathering, perhaps for a charitable cause?" Jill interjected.

"On many occasions." Lizzy responded.

"Then let me ask you this." Bill continued, "Have you ever had to sit at a table at one of those gatherings, maybe at a dinner, with people that you did not know prior to that evening?"

"Sure." Lizzy agreed.

"At the close of the evening, and after chatting with those at your table, didn't you feel at least in a small way that you were somewhat acquainted with them?"

"I guess." Lizzy answered.

"Because of that," Jill interjected. "Many people are found in the Land of Acquaintances. However, few of them make it to the Land of Associates. The reason for this is pretty obvious I'm sure. Bill and I only begin to associate with people with which we have something in common. It might be business, religion, or they could have similar spirits to our own. We might have politics, social, or recreational activities in common, or it could even be something very personal like support groups. There are many reasons of course, but the point that I am trying to make is this, association equals or brings about attachment or detachment, assimilation or elimination."

"What do you mean by that?" Izzy asked.

"I mean that as we associate with some of the people that we have become acquainted with in life, we begin to discover things about them. We make assessments based upon their philosophy of life, their views on issues that we see as important, the manner in which they treat their spouses or those they call friends, the respect demonstrated for others, and well, I guess you get the idea. After the assessment, if we do not feel comfortable with them, their views, or the various positions that they articulate, then we have as a very real option, the choice of no longer associating with them, thereby eliminating them from those in our circle of associates."

Bill interjected, "That means that they never move into our circle of friends. We don't want you to think that this is some type of pure science, because it is not. Sometime it is just a gut level feeling that we cannot place our fingers on, but we've learned to listen to that still small voice that guides us. And we cannot stress the disappointments that we have endured when we did not listen to the urgings of that inner voice that still whispers to each of us when we are confronted with choices or important decisions."

Bill continued, "Let me take a moment and emphasize this in case you missed its importance. Learn to listen to the voice! Learn to trust your gut over your heart. The heart can be emotional; and as emotions go up, logic goes down. Do not dismiss the inner voice; no matter how softly it whispers or loudly it screams. Listen even if it has no audible sound; if it expresses itself in a feeling, a fleeting thought, like something isn't right or is terribly wrong; exit the situation immediately and figure it out later. Listen to this last statement on this subject very carefully. If you ignore that inner-voice, it could be the last thing you never hear again."

Izzy and Lizzy were reeling from the stream of information and its importance when Jill began. "Now listen closely. You asked why there were so few people in the Land of Circle of Friends. There are many answers, but I will at least try to give a few of them. When a person is a friend, and I mean truly a friend, you must be willing to do almost anything in your power for their good. That means that you must be willing to sacrifice the three T's for them. And that is your time, your talent and your treasure, not to mention your life energies."

"Can't you see that you simply cannot have that many people that close to you?" Bill joined in. "The reason is simple, your energies, talents, time, and treasures will continually be drained away from you."

"And believe me; that can seriously damage your relationship with each other and with those in your inner-most circles." Jill added.

Izzy and Lizzy immediately noticed how clearly Bill and Jill were speaking with one voice and one message.

"And think of it in this way." Bill added. "If you and Izzy were batteries with only a limited amount of energy to give, you would soon discover that the more energy that you gave to others, the less you would have left for one another. So Jill and I have made each other the priority in our lives, so we can only afford a few friends. And as you move closer toward the inner circles we will reveal the alternate name for the Lands of Circles. This alternate name will reveal the importance of having only a very few friends. Then you will truly understand why access into these circles must be trusted to only a very few well chosen individuals."

Jill concluded, "Izzy and Lizzy, we hope that you will not misunderstand us. We believe in showing ourselves friendly to everyone, but everyone cannot be our friends."

"Oh I do understand." Izzy smiled.

"So do I." Lizzy agreed.

"If I may speak for both of us," Lizzy continued. "We understand better than you could possibly believe. So many more things that we have done in the past and the negative consequences that followed them are now making so much sense. In fact what you are saying is so logical that I keep asking myself, how is it that we did not see this all sooner."

"Listen, this assessment that Jill spoke about is not a one time thing. It is an ongoing process." Bill smiled warmly. "You must constantly ask yourselves this question again and again, who's in your circles and why."

Jill opened her book to the page where they had last left off. "Are you ready for the next point?" She asked.

"Are we ever?" Izzy and Lizzy responded enthusiastically.

"Let me first repeat something that you both have already learned." Jill stated. "It is rule number five in our personal book. You must never allow anyone inside any of the inner circles unless they respect you, and they must demonstrate that respect through their words and actions. There must be no exceptions to this rule. This might seem nebulous on the surface, but this is incredibly important, because there is a domino affect that will begin to take place immediately. Break this rule, and all other rules will crumble at its side. After a brief pause, Jill added, "Bill will now review our next rule with you."

"Rule number six is this." Bill commenced. When someone, at any level, fails to respect you, they must go back to the outer-most circle or level. That means beyond the outer walls of the Circle of Respect. They must stay there for a good bit of time and earn their way back into your circles one step at a time. Also know this, some people will never be able to re-enter your circles again, for they would have disrespected you in such a way that though you might forgive them, you will discover and acknowledge that it is almost impossible to trust them. It is not that you have an aversion to them or even dislike them. In fact one of the things that have served us best is our decision to never hate or have ill-will toward anyone. The Q-Bugs gave us a quote from John Alberty that revealed the foolishness of such a position. It states, "Hate is a negative energy that holds as it captive the one from whom it emanates." So it is not that you don't like them. It's just that you cannot trust them."

"Rule number seven," Jill began reading. "Keep the levels of communication separate, especially in the presence of a third person. Remember how we discussed in rule two that we should never share information that is on a friend's level with those on the acquaintance's level. We said that violating this rule will quickly lead to serious confusion. This is especially true when two people on the same level are communicating with one another and a third person from a different level enters the conversation."

"If you continue to communicate, let's say on a friend's level to a friend in the presence of an acquaintance, this individual will begin to misunderstand his or her status in the circles. Then this acquaintance may begin to prematurely act and communicate with you on the friend level. You will know when they are doing this because they will say things that make you want to say "Excuse me, what did you say?"

"They will communicate at this level with the expectation that you are going to respond on the friend level every time because you did it during that one instance with your friend while they were present. So it is prudent to communicate with a person only within the circle that you have allowed them into."

"The truth is that we know that rule number seven sounds like rule number two. And in fact it is very similar, but it has the distinction of this third party addition that causes it to be a separate rule." Bill said as he turned the page in the book. "The main concern that gives rise to rule number seven can be stated more succinctly in this manner, a conversation should never go any deeper than the person involved from the outer most circle."

"To illustrate this let's create a scenario. You and Lizzy are at a social gathering chatting and conversing with a friend. The three of you are speaking on the friend's level. While you are talking, a mutual associate, and let me emphasize the word, associate, comes up and joins the conversation. From that point on the conversation between you and your friend should never go deeper than the associate level. In other words, everyone now speaks at the associate level, because to continue to speak at the friend level with an associate present, could give the associate a false impression of his status with you."

"The problem with associates believing themselves to be friends when they are not creates a good potential for injured feelings. Believe it or not, you will have to eventually put that associate in his or her proper place or further violate your own rules."

Izzy and Lizzy were amazed at how much sense these principles made. They were so pure and felt so right to the both of them. "That is enough for this evening." Jill smiled. "Let's relax and enjoy the time we have left."

The evening passed quickly and so did the time with the Special Ones. Izzy and Lizzy grew in knowledge and their relationship with each other grew by leaps and bounds. Their relationship with the Special Ones had also grown more endearing.

CHAPTER TEN
A Lesson in the Trees

Months went by as Izzy and Lizzy interacted with Jill and Bill, but this day was somehow going to be different. Izzy sensed it in his soul, but he couldn't quite put his finger on it. It was a cool fall day; at least it appeared to be fall. One could never really tell what season it was in the Lands of Circles, because it was always exceptional weather there.

The leaves were simply phenomenal as they cooperated with nature to form a kaleidoscope of colors that danced with the movement and energy of darting breezes. In a tenuous and fragile affair the wind wrestled with the giant branches for possession of the leaves. In this setting Izzy stood alone watching the struggle in the trees when Lizzy came up and tapped him on the shoulder.

"Hi honey, what are you staring at?" She asked as she peered in the same direction as Izzy.

"Oh it's nothing and yet it seems like everything. It's just so beautiful out here and I was watching the trees contend with the wind. I think that I have figured something out that will make our relationship even more special."

165

"What is it?" Lizzy asked.

Izzy took Lizzy by the hand and led her inside. He pulled a chair away from the table and positioned it in front of the large window. He then took a second chair and placed it next to the first. "Have a seat." Izzy whispered softly with a smile. As Lizzy sat down, Izzy sat next to her. "I wanted you to come inside for just a moment, because I do not want anything to distract you or take away from what I am about to share with you."

"What is it?" Lizzy anxiously asked.

"Do me a small favor and look through the window at the trees." After a brief pause Izzy continued. "Look closer and pay very close attention to the leaves. Do you see how the wind blows against them and seems to almost wrestle with the trees for the possession of each leaf?"

"I never thought of it like that before." Lizzy responded softly as she experienced Izzy's epiphany.

"You're probably asking yourself right now, what this could be leading to." Izzy offered. "I guess I could answer by saying that it leads down several roads. Lizzy, I was thinking about how wonderful everything has been in our lives and in our relationship since we

166

found one another. But what happens when the wind blows?" Izzy paused for an answer.

"Are you asking is our relationship storm proof?" Lizzy replied as she directed her eyes to his.

"No sweetie, I believe with all of my heart that it is storm proof, but I noticed that the wintry blast wreaks havoc on the leafy trees, but not the pine trees. The leafy trees are beautiful in the spring and summer time, but the pine also endures the harshness of winter as well as the other seasons. I believe that you and I are like the pine trees. Should the winter blast ever blow our way, I know in my heart that we will endure. This means that our relationship cannot change with the seasons. Nor can it change to accommodate the challenging situations or the people around us. It must be steadfast and consistent."

"Let's say that the cold and wind represent people who are antagonistic to our relationship; I mean those who would purposely try to damage our relationship. It is important that we are insulated against them. That is why we are here, to learn how to love and protect one another. This is a preparation time for what is to surely come."

Buzz came a sound of wisdom in the Q-Bugs. "If you have eight hours to chop a tree, you should spend seven hours sharpening your axe. Abraham Lincoln."

"And that is what we are doing Lizzy. We are sharpening our axes to cut through the obstacles that life will surely bring to our doorsteps."

"There was another point that came to my mind as I considered the leaves wrestling in the wind. I have come to the conclusion that it is such a small event that no one really notices it. We see all of the dead leaves on the ground, but seldom do we pay attention to the wind severing their ties to the branches of the trees. All of this made me want to tell you that nothing is too small. I want to pay attention to the minute details of your life. Anything that matters to you, I want it to matter to me. What you have to say will always be important to me. In essence I want you to know that I hear you. Listen." Izzy continued as he softly placed his finger on Lizzy's lips.

"I hope to always listen to what these two lips have to say. I guess what I'm trying to say is that you matter. What you have to say matters. I want you to know that I will hold on to every one of your words. I will be like those few remaining leaves wrestling in the wind that will not give up, give in, give out, or let go."

"You know what?" Lizzy taunted Izzy.

"What is that?" Izzy questioned.

"I guess the Special Ones aren't the only ones with wisdom." Izzy and Lizzy embraced and held on to each other and they also held on to that moment as a single point in time that would always be incredibly special. They agreed, that from that day forward, every time they witnessed or took notice of a leaf in its struggle with the wind to maintain its position on a branch, they would remember the lessons learned on this day. They would silently say to the leaf and to themselves, "Hang in there, hold on, hold up, and hold out, because we can do it! We have the power, the knowledge, and the will of an indomitable spirit that cannot be broken.

WHO'S IN YOUR CIRCLES

CHAPTER ELEVEN
A Major Lesson on a Circle Beyond the Circles

The Circle of the Land of Friends had been an amazing experience for Izzy and Lizzy. Today had begun with an early breakfast at Lizzy's cottage. The menu included fresh fruits and other freshly selected foods that were native to the Lands of Circles. Izzy loved the snozzle berries. They had become his favorite treats. They were tart and they warmed up when you placed them in your mouth. He liked the fact that they were cold to start with, because it made the warming action more pronounced and enjoyable. He would not chew with his teeth or move his tongue until the warmth was just right.

Izzy really didn't know the name of the great tasting berries, but he named them snozzle berries because they looked like the miniature snouts of elephants' trunks. Lizzy never fully understood the connection, but she also called them snozzle berries.

"Delicious." Came the compliment from a lip smacking Izzy to Lizzy. "You make the best snozzle berries I have ever tasted."

"But all I do is place them in a bowl. They don't even require washing."

"Like I said," Izzy continued with a smile, "You make the best snozzle berries I have ever tasted." They both laughed aloud.

Thump! Thump! Thump! It was an unexpected banging sound indicating the presence of someone or something at the door. Thump! Thump! Thump! The sound came again with a certain hint that someone was being impatient, or something was urgent. Izzy rushed to open the door not knowing what to expect.

"It's time." The coachman nervously commented, almost stuttering as he pointed to the open door of the coach. "Hurry! You must hurry. It's time." He repeated.

"Time for what?" Lizzy asked almost as nervously as the coachman. "There was no invitation to visit the Special Ones." Quickly turning toward Izzy she inquired, "Did you get an invitation?"

"No sweetie." Izzy responded somewhat stressfully.

"There is a time and a season for everything under the sun." The coachman responded. "It's time, and we must all hurry! The Special Ones require your presence immediately. The coachman added as he hastily trotted toward the open door of the coach.

"Wait a second." Izzy called out as he took Lizzy by the hand and she concomitantly grabbed the door knob slamming the door shut as she and Izzy ran and clambered into the coach.

Izzy and Lizzy held hands tightly. They were a bit tense, even though they both knew that a brand new journey had begun. They sensed that something was even more pressing and special about this departure, because it did not come with a formal invitation or any forewarning, as they had always received before their prior travels.

When the carriage sat down, they immediately sensed that this was not the Lands of Circles. Everything was so different. "Where are we?" Lizzy asked the coachman, but when she turned to look for an answer, Izzy and Lizzy discovered that they were alone. The coach and coachman had vanished without a sound, without a word, and without a trace.

Crack! It was a sound that seemed to come from the other side of a very large boulder. "Did you hear that?" Izzy asked as he and Lizzy moved closer together to calm each other.

"Info-Bugs." Lizzy called out and waited, but there was no response.

"My," Izzy quipped. "I guess we really have left the Lands of Circles."

"Yes." Lizzy whispered. "Crack." It was the loud noise again. Izzy and Lizzy moved still closer toward each other as Izzy protectively took Lizzy into his arms. "Do not be afraid." Izzy asserted softly to calm Lizzy. "I will go and investigate." He valiantly proclaimed.

"Wait! Do you think that we should just leave?" Lizzy timidly whispered.

"I don't know if we should move toward it or run from it." An honest Izzy whispered even softer.

Izzy began to ease forward while motioning for Lizzy to hold her position. But Lizzy closely followed as she whispered to Izzy, "Our strength is in our togetherness."

Izzy momentarily paused and looked into her eyes, after giving her an assuring smile, they both slowly made their way toward the other side of the stone. They were very surreptitious as they peered over the top and around the side of the huge boulder. "Hello." Bill and Jill called out from a short distance.

"Listen." Bill began immediately explaining. "I know that this was all very sudden, but Jill and I had no idea that the Land of a Different Circle would open its portal so soon. We rushed here and had another coach to come for you. This portal only opens about once every six months."

"You see," Jill interjected. "We have both agreed that maybe it is time for you to move on, but there are things that you must absolutely know first. And these things can only be taught from the Land of a Different Circle. Please take a seat there." Jill suggested pointing to a pre-agreed upon spot that she and Bill had hastily prepared for Izzy and Lizzy's arrival.

"We did take a brief moment to pack some food because we did not know if you would have had time to eat." Bill stated while sitting down.

"We're fine for now." Lizzy responded with Izzy shaking his head in agreement.

"Alright then let's get started." Bill heaved aside a large tarp like covering of heavy plastic. It had apparently been put into place in order to hide the view of what appeared to be some type of large and strange glass portal. "You will see people and things that do not exist

175

except for the purpose of the lessons to be taught. This is known as In-Vivo-Vision." Bill stated as he stared into the open face of the glassy looking prism. "Each person sees images that are generated by their own minds. It is exactly what they are thinking relative to what is being discussed. However, I cannot see your vision, nor can you see mine. We can only see what is in our own minds. It is our own thoughts that give the In-Vivo-Vision its energy."

"You have heard it said that a picture is worth a thousand words. The In-Vivo-Vision allows us to teach you in minutes what would normally take weeks or even months to learn." Jill smiled. "Are you ready to begin?"

Izzy and Lizzy nodded in agreement as they looked down into the In-Vivo-Vision which looked more like a large perfectly shaped crystal clear and translucent stone that was half buried and set in a larger golden stone that seemed to glow all around it.

"In a minute," Jill smiled. "We'll look at the In-Vivo-Vision in just a minute." She repeated. "But first we must make sure that you understand that you are now in the Land of a Different Circle. There are no Info-Bugs, but it is filled with Q-Bugs. This is the land of their origin. As you know there will be a very brief buzzing sound. When you hear it, please be sure to listen ever so carefully."

"Do not be alarmed at the difference here in this land. When the Q-Bugs arrive, two distinct things will quickly happen. They will hastily cite a quote without any warning other than the brief buzzing sound. They will not introduce themselves here, for it is not customary for them to do so. This is their home. Secondly, when you hear the buzz, do not be alarmed when Bill and I become totally suspended in a sort of frozen animation. Because they are speaking exclusively to the two of you, we cannot hear or see them, and we cannot move or talk as long as they are present. We will begin speaking exactly where we left off when they leave." Jill stated.

Bill added, "We will never know that they were here unless you tell us. Jill and I do not know why the portal hole opened when it did. We only know that it can close at any time and usually does so without any signs. However, once we are here, we can always leave. With the portal hole it is about the entering and not the exiting. I can tell you this much, before you and Lizzy leave here, you will both know why you had to be here at this particular time. The lessons taught here are for you."

"By the way, once you have learned why you came here, you are not allowed to tell us. The Land of a Different Circle is a lesson uniquely for the two of you. Do you understand?" Bill asked with a sense of urgency registering in his voice.

"I think so." Izzy cautiously responded.

"Do not be alarmed. It's just that we are not here for ourselves. That is all that we are trying to say. We are here with you and for you. Everything that happens here in this place is about you and for your growth." Bill smiled.

"Let's begin." Jill encouraged. "When this experience has passed, the next land that you will approach, if you continue to progress, in the Lands of Circles is a very favorable land. I say if you progress only to keep you aware of the real possibility that things can go wrong and that there is no guarantee that you will make it any further than the land in which you presently reside."

"This knowledge will keep you from becoming too comfortable and letting your guard down. I can tell you now, that should you reach the next land in the Lands of Circles, you will see very few individuals there."

"The reason should be obvious to you by now." Izzy and Lizzy could hear a sense of urgency and determination in Bill's voice that they had not heard before. Bill continued, "You are here because we are very seriously considering inviting you into our very small circle that lies just ahead of this land. And before Jill and I could do that there are other aspects of friendship to be considered. You and Lizzy must do the same thing before you allow anyone to move into your very special inner circles, where only very few must exist if you are to exist as a couple."

"Remember." Jill cut in, "When you allow someone into your most inner circles, you are giving entrance to all of their strengths and talents, but also all of their weaknesses and baggage. We will talk about the origin of that baggage later."

"That baggage can be anything." Bill admitted. "And I do mean anything. That is why you keep people outside of the close friend circle until you have had ample opportunities to observe them under various circumstances and conditions; particularly trying conditions, where true character is revealed."

Buzz came the sound of the Q-Bugs. "May Sarton says that instant intimacy is very often followed by desperate disillusion."

"If we let individuals in too quickly," Bill continued, not knowing that he had been frozen momentarily along with Jill in the presence of the Q-Bugs. "Then we have to deceive ourselves. Let me give you an example. You allow, let's say, Bob and Barbara into your circle of close friends. They then end up violating some of the very core rules of friendship. And now you and Lizzy find yourselves in disbelief saying things like, I cannot believe they did that. How could they violate our friendship like that? When the truth is really this, true close friends would not have committed such an act."

"Now you must delude yourselves by telling yourselves that you cannot believe that your close friends treated you like that. When in reality, they were never your friends nor were they your close friends. Therefore, you must delude yourselves because you cannot handle the cold hard truth. And that truth is that you made an error in judgment. You allowed your emotions to govern your decisions to allow them entrance into your inner circles. That is the conduct of a child, not an adult."

"Listen closely," Jill began. "Never make a decision based upon emotions. Here is a fact about emotions that to a small degree we attempted to teach earlier. When emotions go up, rational thinking goes down. They are dichotomously opposed and inversely proportioned. Never invite anyone into any of your circles based on emotions. It must be a rational decision and only done after extensive observation."

Buzz came the sound of the Q-Bugs again as they repeated themselves, which was something that was seldom done. "May Sarton says, that instant intimacy is very often followed by desperate disillusion."

"When you do not observe individuals long enough," Jill continued. "You will see only what they want you to see. Everyone can wear a social mask, which is also known as a persona. But a person requires a great deal of psyche or mental energy to maintain that persona for any extensive period of time. In essence, a person will become neurotic trying to keep a persona in place for too long a period of time."

"Therefore, in your protracted observation of others, if they are being pretentious with a spurious or specious persona in place; it will surface and be exposed if you are attentive to details. You will soon see flaws or cracks being revealed in their character. What they say will not equate to what they do. That inner-voice, if not silenced, will alert you." Jill stressed.

"What makes this pretentiousness or phoniness so unacceptable is that the solution is so simple. All people have to do is be themselves and stop playing games. Your responsibility is to observe them until you believe that what you are seeing is who they really are. Violate this rule of observation and you will only have yourselves to indict for the destructive consequences that will surely follow. In short, observe, observe, observe, and investigate, investigate, investigate!"

Buzz came the sound of the Q-Bugs. "Confucius says, "No investigation, no right to speak."

"If you invite individuals into you inner-most circles and they abuse your trust, then you have no one to blame but yourselves. And to be frank, what right do you have to complain and say that you cannot believe the wrong they did to you, when in reality the cold hard truth is that it is the wrong that you did to yourselves. You failed to keep them in the outer circles long enough to properly investigate them. Had you done so, you would have had a much better chance of seeing them for who they really were and concomitantly protecting yourselves." Jill continued.

"Once someone has injured you, there is something that you must remember. In relationships that have had problems and where injuries have occurred people build walls. And as relationships mend they will not be prepared to quickly tear those walls down. However, as they continue to mend they may begin to slowly tear the walls down. But you must remember that these walls will not, and should not come down too quickly because they were built for protection and defense against further injury." Bill asserted.

"Listen." Jill interjected. "Let me repeat that, until that person feels safe they will not, nor should they tear the walls down. The injured party has a serious choice to make. It should not be based on pleasing people, but self protection. Tear the wall down too quickly and the consequences can be dire for that choice. However, there is a fine balance. The injured party cannot become a hermit and move into an ascetic shell. They have a choice to make." Jill concluded.

"It's all about choices and consequences." Bill stated. "Let me repeat that. It's all about choices and consequences. The process of making a choice is a simple one, but only if you have goals and plans. By the way, you do not allow people into your inner circles that do not make choices based on goal oriented plans. If I have goal oriented plans, then I know where I want to go with my life. I have it mapped out. I have a strategy for getting there."

"Now you might ask how does this help in making choices. Well, let's put it like this. When I come to a point in my life where I have to make a choice, I simply hold my right hand out to the right, which represents the choice that will move me toward my goal and my left hand out to the left, which represents the choice that will move me away from my goal. If I am goal driven, the choice is easy. I simply ask myself is this choice going to move me closer to my goal or away from my goal. I then make the decision that is going to move me closer to my objective or goal. If there is more than one choice in my right hand, then I make the one that will give me greater impetus toward my desired goal. The people in your inner circles simply must be goal and objective driven."

Listen closely." Jill implored. "Some people take this power of choice thing lightly, but it is the core of everything. The truth might frighten you, but the fact is this; the power of choice is all that we really have."

"Huh?" Izzy asked.

"Name something that you believe we have other than the power of choice." Jill challenged Izzy and Lizzy.

"People own their homes." Izzy suggested. "Do they?" Jill asked rhetorically. "When they die, what happens to the home? Can they take it with them? No, they cannot. They are only stewards for their brief journey through this experience that we call life. Let me ask you this question. What did you have when you were born? In essence what did you come into this world with?"

"Nothing really." Lizzy answered after a short pause.

"And that is just what we are going to leave here with, nothing." Jill stated emphatically.

"Well how about our bodies?" Izzy responded.

"Not even our bodies are ours." Jill answered. "If we truly own them or had absolute power over them, we would not allow them to age after a certain point, or become diseased, sick, overweight, or filled with pain. Our bodies at best are just temporary structures created by the Author of the universe. They are for us to occupy and a way for us to interact with our environment and one another. They are mere dwelling places for who we really are. When these bodies are used up they too, like every thing else, will return to the earth from which they were borrowed."

"We own nothing except the power of choice. And understanding this essential principle is a crucial key to figuring out life itself, because the choices we make should be those that give us more choices, not less. Think about it; not having a choice is oppressive and depressive. In fact it is probably the central cause of depression as we know it." Jill expounded.

"Listen, I believe that one day people will discover that depression is only a symptom of losing control over certain aspects of one's life. The exception to this is when depression is caused purely or in part by physiological factors such as chemical or hormonal imbalances. This depression, which is caused by a lack of control over one's life, is about individuals who have choices that they desire to make, but their desired choices are no longer available or are no longer viable options that they have to choose from."

"What do you mean by that?" Lizzy asked.

"Think for a moment, what are some of the things that people become depressed over? Name as many as you can as quickly as you can." Jill waited for their answers.

"Some things are the death of a loved one, loss of love, divorce, overwhelming indebtedness, children or loved ones being sick, or a person's own sickness." Izzy and Lizzy alternated their answers before being cut off by Jill.

"Now let's say that just by making a choice that a person could reverse the death of a loved one and bring that person back to life, would they still be depressed over that matter?"

I guess not." Izzy answered.

"Well," Jill continued. "What if they could by their choices regain loss love, get rid of all of their debt, make their marriage work or cure their children or themselves, would they be depressed?

"I guess not if you put it like that." Lizzy said thoughtfully.

"Don't you see," Jill continued. "Choices represent the control that we have over our lives. Depression is a symptom of a loss of that control. It is imperative that we make choices that liberate us and give us more choices or more control over our own lives. This is extremely important for those allowed into our inner circles, because when they limit their choices by having previously made poor choices, depression will be a pervasive part of their lives, and if they are in your inner-most circles, you can believe that their depression will definitely impact you negatively."

"So what Jill is saying," Bill interposed. "You must not allow people into your inner circles who do not have plans for their lives that are driven by goals. Because if they are absent of goal oriented plans their choices will have no real foundations and will be based on the way they feel or are thinking at that moment. Those types of choices will haphazardly take them here, there, and then nowhere."

"Choices without goals are done without thought of where one wants to be in the distant future. They are more reactive than proactive and only serve to limit future choices. And if we follow this pattern of behavior to its natural conclusion, the choices will become more and more limited until there are no choices. This will then lead to a lack of control over their lives, which will then lead to depression, which will cause them to become dysfunctional and stressed."

"Can you give an example?" Izzy asked.

"Certainly." Jill responded. Let's consider the person who chooses to drop out of high school and not get a diploma or GED. They have just made a choice that will limit their future choices. Tech school, colleges and universities and all the technical and professional based jobs that they bring with them are no longer viable choices that they have available to them. Let's say that this person chooses also to do drugs. With almost all jobs demanding drug-free work places, their choices are further limited. If they are arrested for this drug-based behavior, they now have a criminal record, and their choices are even further limited. If a person continues to make limiting choices, they will eventually find themselves frustrated, depressed, angry, dejected, and choiceless."

"Why angry?" Izzy asked.

"There are several reasons." Bill answered. "Let's say that this person now has to work at jobs that they literally hate, but these jobs are all that they are qualified to do. And let's add that this person is a relatively intelligent person who made poor choices because they honestly did not know better, or because they felt that those choices were the only ones available."

"At any rate they are intelligent and feel that they can do much more than the responsibility given to them. However, because of their previous choices they are passed over time and time again for promotions that are going to people who are less qualified experience wise, and who are only better qualified by their education. This person may become angry with himself, and may become self-destructive or he might eventually turn that anger outward toward others and become destructive toward them."

"So the choices we make today can be empowering or limiting to our future and future choices." Izzy commented.

"Absolutely." Jill and Bill replied.

"Let me see if I can highlight a little of what was just stated." Izzy asserted with confidence.

1. Choices are based upon goal oriented plans.

2. If a choice is going to move me toward my goal, I make that choice.

3. If a choice is going to move me away from my goal, I do not make that choice.

4. Choices should be made that increase the number of options or choices available in the future, and give a person more control of their own lives.

5. The lack of choices can be a major cause of depression based on feelings of powerlessness and frustration.

6. Good choices empower us toward our desired destinations." Izzy concluded.

"That was very good Izzy." A supportive Lizzy cheered.

"Remember this simple line." Jill interjected. "Choices are destinations!"

"And some choices can be permanent destinations." Bill added. "Understand that the reason that we are spending so much time on this subject of choice is because it is that important. If you have anyone in your inner circles who make poor choices; they will eventually have few to no choices. You will be their choice and they will impose upon and inconvenience you on a regular basis. They will too often have a fire to put out somewhere."

With that verbalized, Bill and Jill gave Izzy and Lizzy two hand-held mirrors that were located near them. "Look into them." Jill instructed.

When they both were looking into their own mirrors, Bill repeated, "Like I said, they will always have a fire to put out somewhere, and in case you do not already know it, let Jill and I be the first to tell you, that the both of you are looking at their firemen in the mirror. The lack of their planning will too often be your emergencies. You simply cannot afford to have people like that in your inner circles. Now let's dig deeper into how and why people make the choices they make.

WHO'S IN YOUR CIRCLES

CHAPTER TWELVE
How and Why People Make the Choices They Make

"Are you ready for the next lesson?" Bill smiled.

"This is all going so fast." An anxious Izzy sighed."

"Don't worry." Bill assured him. Everything that you learn in this Special Land of a Different Circle will be fully integrated into your memory. I don't know how it happens, but it does."

"Great! Then let's go." Lizzy prompted.

"Our focus is centered on how and why people make the choices they make. It is important that you know the answer to this, and though it will take a good deal of time to examine the nuances, it will absolutely be worth it. This means that we must explore the avenues of the mind and how those avenues work."

Bill continued, "First let's look into the In-Vivo-Vision. Remember we may see different things, but each of us will see what we need to see in order to get a clear understanding of what is being discussed."

"On rare occasions, we will all observe the same thing." Jill interjected. "But what Bill is saying is that, such a singular observation where we are all seeing the identical same thing is not usually the case." With that spoken they all looked into the In-Vivo-

193

Vision and this is what they saw in various presentations shaped by their own minds.

There were eight figures that appeared to be people. These figures surrounded a young lady who sat in a chair in the center of them. The young lady was obviously filled with fear and duress. Each figure was screaming and shouting at the young lady.

When Lizzy looked closer, each of the figures surrounding the young lady had a metal bar in their hand. Working together they had formed a cage or jail cell around the young lady. She tried harder and harder to escape the cell, but she could not. In fact, Lizzy could see her as she weakened more and more beneath the unending stream of shouts and screams.

Lizzy desperately wanted to know what they were saying to her that had such great power to weaken the young lady so much. The very moment that Lizzy had the thought of desiring to understand what they were saying; she could clearly hear their every word. One figure screamed, "You can't do that; you're not smart enough."

Another shouted, "If you try and fail everyone will laugh at you."

The third yelled, "Remember the last time. Remember your wrongs. You deserve punishment not success."

The fourth whispered, "You don't have enough money to do that."

The fifth shouted, "Wait on the Lord, any way, are you sure that God wants that for you?"

The sixth followed, "You don't have enough training or education, and there are so many more people who are much smarter than you."

The seventh called out, "You have too many other obligations."

The eighth simply laughed the young lady to scorn and then they all screamed in unison over and over again, "You don't deserve it so you will not get it."

"That's horrible." Lizzy voiced in disbelief.

"The nerve of those people or things or whatever they are." Izzy joined in as if he had seen images similar to those that Lizzy had seen.

"Don't let what you saw or might see upset you." Jill spoke in a soft and calming voice. "You will see much more than that. Some of what you see will make you want to cry. Other things will make you want to laugh, and still others will make you angry, but remember that when emotions go up, logic or rational thinking goes down. And remember too, that whatever it is that you are feeling emotionally, you are contributing to those feelings with your own thinking."

Izzy and Lizzy reflected on what was spoken and then quickly told what they had seen. "It was nerve-racking and stressful." Lizzy commented as she ended her commentary on what she had witnessed.

"I want to place what you just saw, though it might have been slightly different for Bill and me, into the proper perspective, or a more dramatic light." Jill began.

"Those figures with the bars were the young lady's own thoughts. They could just as easily have represented our thoughts. It was really most revealing. What it was saying in its own way was that we are actually the prisoners of our own minds or more specifically our own thoughts! Henry Ford said, "If you think you can or can't, you're right!"

Buzz came the Q-Bugs, "Aerodynamically, the bumble bee shouldn't be able to fly, but the bumble bee doesn't know it so it goes on flying anyway. Mary Kay Ash"

"Listen, thinking makes it so! There is a whole field of psychology known as cognitive-behavior therapy, cognitive restructuring, and Rational Emotive Therapy that is based almost entirely upon this single concept, thinking makes it so." Bill interjected.

Jill followed. "Our minds didn't just happen. The young lady thoughts didn't just pop up out of nowhere. There is a reason she thinks the way that she does. Believe it or not, we are all the products of the thinking or workings of our minds. In essence, we are what we believe ourselves to be. And since we are the products of our minds, thoughts and our thinking, then shouldn't we ask ourselves another question?"

Bill began, "If we are the products of our minds and thoughts, then what are our minds and thoughts the products of? In essence, why do we think what we think? Listen, what do you think makes our thinking what it is? The answer to this single question will give us an insight so deep that we will have much better control and power over who enters our circles. And it will also give greater insight as to why they should or should not be in them"

"How is that?" Izzy asked.

"Well if we do not know why we think the way that we do, then even what appears to be rational thoughts to us, could in fact be acutely or terribly irrational. And if we are thinking irrationally, we could, to our own detriment, allow negative and destructive forces deep into our inner most circles." Jill answered.

"Now back to the question, why do we think the way that we do?" Bill interjected. "The answer to this question will also give us insight into why and how the young lady's thoughts were controlling her to the point that they actually had the power to mentally imprison her. This answer is also important because millions upon millions are being imprisoned by their own minds on a day-to-day basis without having a clue as to how they can escape from their enemy; because what they do not realize is that they themselves have joined the ranks of the enemy; doubting almost every possibility of their greatness and therefore insuring their own failure."

Buzz came the entrance of the Q-Bugs, "A person who doubts himself is like a man who would enlist in the ranks of his enemies and bear arms against himself. He makes his failure certain by himself being the first person to be convinced of it. – Alexander Dumas"

Bill continued without any awareness of the quotation of the Q-Bugs, "And what is so devastating is that most people are not remotely conscious of their prisoner status."

"Look into the In-Vivo-Vision." Jill directed Izzy and Lizzy. "This will take us back a little ways in earth's history. There was a time that people believed that children were born being fundamentally evil. They were thought to be born with the label "bad", with malevolent minds overflowing with evil. This was known as the *Original Sin View*. The entire focus of parental guidance was the salvation of the child. In essence the parents thought that their fundamental goal was to deliver the child from his or her evil state of sinfulness; lead him to salvation and ultimately save his or her life."

"That was followed in the 18th century, by Jean-Jacques Rousseau's theory of *Innate Goodness*." Bill asserted. "This view postured that children were born with little halos. It promoted that they were basically good and very little guidance was needed because they would naturally do the right things because of their basic goodness."

"The theory of John Locke was born later. He tendered the proposition that children are innately neither good nor bad. Locke believed that the minds of children were blank tablets so to speak. He called his approach "Tabula Rasa" or the blank tablet. In essence, we start life with a blank tablet or mind, upon which life immediately begins to write each experience and thereto attach feelings."

"Listen." Jill added. "Because here rests the key phrase. Locke stated that children acquire their characteristics through their life experiences. Of course this is not about children, but the very nature of how our minds develop. I am talking about how things got into our minds in the first place. The tabula rasa view says that everything was written there by our experiences. This is the view that Bill and I believe to be correct."

"So then," Bill interjected. "If we are what we think, and what we think is the product of our experiences, then we are the products of our experiences. I believe that this merits repeating. If we are what we think we are, and what we think is the product of our experiences, then we are the products of our experiences. In essence, what we are is what life experiences have made us into. And it is these very experiences that have shaped our thinking." Everyone saw this formula in their In-Vivo-Vision.

```
            IF A = B AND B = C
               THEN A = C
IF EXPERIENCES = THOUGHTS AND THOUGHTS = US
    THEN OUR EXPERIENCES = WHO WE ARE
```

"And here's the kicker." Jill continued. The majority of these foundational life experiences, that have made us who we are, were written on our blank slates while we were young children. And get this; "Development of the frontal regions of the brain is known to continue through late adolescence and into early adulthood" (Romine & Reynolds, 2005). This is critical to understand, because this is the part of the brain that is vital to judgment, self-control and reasoning."

Jill continued, "And because most of these foundational experiences occurred prior to the full development of the prefrontal cortex, while we were immature and trusting children, it was impossible for these experiences to be critically assessed for accuracy, worth, and value as they happened to us. This is very imperative to note. A good part of this information and the accompanying emotions were placed in our minds by experiences with significant others. We more than likely just accepted what they had to say as fact, because they were significant to us. We accepted this without any critical assessment, as to the status of the information as facts."

"At the very best there was only minimal assessing. And these un-assessed, un-analyzed, and un-critiqued thoughts are right now, at this moment, controlling not only you and me, but billions of other people who have never taken the time to challenge their validity. Don't you see, most of us never challenged their validity because they were placed there before any of us ever had the ability to critically study, investigate, or analyze their legitimacy, validity, correctness, or soundness." Asserted Jill.

"These thoughts entered our minds because of the experiences that we have gone through; experiences that have been channeled through one of our fives senses of hearing, smelling, seeing, touching, or tasting. This also includes inter-modal experiences. This simply means that it might be something that aroused two or more senses at the same time. An example would be something that we might have seen and heard at the same time."

"Stay with me," Jill encouraged. "Now as we have these experiences, we attach emotional tags that tell us if these experiences are either good, neutral, or bad. Those experiences that we perceive as good, from a behavioral aspect, are more likely to be repeated by us."

"As we repeat these behaviors more and more, they become habits. It is these habits that form what is known as behavioral patterns or patterns of behavior."

Buzz, it was the Q-Bugs, "We are what we repeatedly do. Excellence then is not an act but a habit." Aristotle.

"As these patterns of behavior are observed by others who observe us, they then characterize us according to these behavior patterns. Let me give a few examples. If a person develops a behavior of telling lies, we characterize that person as a liar. If a person is observed gossiping a lot, we characterized that person as a gossiper." Jill stated.

"Yes." Bill agreed then continued. "Once a person is characterized, then we develop expectations of that person based upon those characterizations. Let's continue with our previous example. If a person is characterized as a liar, then we expect him or her to lie. In fact, it is very hard to believe anything that he or she might say, because we expect them to lie almost every time they open their mouth."

Another example of this is the classic Aesop Fable of "The Boy Who Cried Wolf." He was expected to call the villagers if a wolf came near the sheep that he was assigned to watch. He called out wolf several times and when the town people came rushing to attack the wolf to keep it from attacking the sheep, they found that the boy was lying. He did this repeatedly until the wolf really did show up. The boy cried wolf, but no one responded."

"The key point in this story is the fact that on the last occasion the boy was actually telling the truth. However, no one believed him. Can you tell me why?" Jill asked.

"I can." Lizzy volunteered as she directed her attention from the In-Vivo-Vision, where she had watched everything being discussed unfold. "The reason that no one believed him is because he had been characterized as a liar, and even when the boy told the truth, the people kept him within the context of their characterization, which is that of a liar."

"Yes," Izzy added. "Characterization is sort of like a box that you are placed in by others. Once the box is labeled, no matter what the present behavior is, the people still see you according to the label on the box."

"That's correct." Bill responded. "In fact, Carl Rogers, the founder of Person-Centered Therapy, and other psychologists believe that we are what others expect us to be. This means that many people are living out their lives, to a very large extent, to the expectations of other people."

"So a great deal of what we have just said has been done to emphasize that you cannot let people into your inner circles who are unwilling to reexamine their unfounded values, beliefs, and assumptions. Their ability to do this will insure that they are true or congruent to who they are and what they desire to become. Individuals who cannot change and who refuse to re-examine why they are as they are will be inflexible, and inflexible people are definitely not the type of people that you want within your inner circles."

Buzz came the sound of the Q-Bugs, "The illiterate of the 21st century will not be those who cannot read and write, but those who cannot learn, unlearn, and relearn. Alvin Toffler."

"What most people do not fully comprehend," Bill began. "Is that when a person changes their basic schema or thought pattern, they are no longer the same person. Listen, we are our thoughts! How we think is who we are or who we are becoming. So if we can change our mind, our attitude or reframe the way we think, then we become the product of those new thoughts."

Buzz came the noise of the Q-Bugs. "Nothing has changed but my attitude, therefore, everything has changed. Anthony Demello."

"Let's quickly review what we have just articulated." Jill emphasized as she began the review.

1. We are born into this world with minds that are like blank tablets.

2. Through our five senses, we have various experiences that begin to write upon our blank tablet.

3. We have different emotions that are attached to these different experiences. We see them as positive, negative, or neutral.

4. These emotions or feelings and their related experiences form the basis of our thoughts.

5. These thoughts cause us to behave in a certain way, therefore our thoughts lead to our behaviors.

6. We will usually repeat those behaviors that we perceived as positive, or for which we are positively reinforced.

7. Those repeated behaviors lead to patterns of behavior or habits.

8. Patterns of behavior lead to characterizations by others.

9. These characterizations by others lead to expectations by them.

Depending upon our view of these others, we will live out our lives trying to live up to their expectations. This is particularly true if we hold them in high esteem or ourselves in low esteem. This is especially the case if both conditions exist.

10. So in essence, far too often, we are living the lives that others are expecting us to live, and not our own lives as they are based on our own interpretation of the world or our own worldview.

11. And we are doing this largely based upon input or experiences that came into our minds at a very early age, before we were capable of critically analyzing if this information from others, or our childhood experiences was valid or sound.

12. Living out the expectations of others, which are contrary to our own beliefs, will lead to incongruency between our thoughts and actions, which can contribute to disturbing behaviors.

"Well where do others get their expectations from?" Lizzy asked in an almost rhetorical manner.

"They get them from the same place that we do." Bill smiled. "They get them from their experiences."

"Wait a minute." Izzy was having an epiphany. "So we are the products of the expectations of others. They became who they are based upon the expectations of others. Therefore, we are living out our lives based one, on our own experiences and two, the expectations of others. However, it goes much deeper than those others. Our lives are not just based on the experiences and expectations of these other people, but also those who they got their thoughts, experiences, and expectations from. This continues to the generation before them, who in turn got their thoughts from the generation before them, and even before them and etcetera, etcetera, etcetera."

"You've got it!" Jill responded before continuing. "Bringing this to its logical conclusion, if we do not continually examine and re-examine our thoughts for accuracy and validity, we will forever be the puppets of generations of puppeteers and their thoughts. This includes even the skewed and warped thoughts, experiences and expectations of those who are dead and buried. Their ancient views of the world still live on through the minds of those who have absorbed them over generations."

"I told you," sighed an almost exhausted Jill, "that this would get deep. But at this level you must understand that the people that you allow into your inner circles must be independent thinkers, because here's another kicker. If they are not, then you are not only allowing that person into your inner circle, but coming in with them is the army or generations of puppeteers that presently continue to pull their strings; and in effect through them, pull your strings."

It should be clear, if people come into your outer most circles with all kinds of strings attached or a whole lot of baggage, that they do not belong in your inner circles. I want everyone to repeat after me only if you are so inclined." Bill prompted. "I will not allow anyone to define my reality; not even the master puppeteers from the past."

They all repeated after Bill. "I will not allow anyone to define my reality."

"The only way that this can happen is that we set boundaries. So if you are inclined to do so repeat these words with me." Bill again prompted. "If we do not set boundaries for ourselves, other people will. And we will end up doing the will of other people. And we must refuse to do the will of other people, when it is not in our best interest."

They all loudly repeated, "If we do not set boundaries for ourselves, other people will. And we will end up doing the will of other people. And we must refuse to do the will of other people, when it is not in our best interest."

"Listen," an enthusiastic Bill exclaimed. "Jill and I have a simple rule about doing other people's will. Usually when someone operates in a mode of trying to control you, and impose or attempt to impose their will on you; it is because they are attempting to satisfy their own personal needs. I wouldn't go so far as labeling them as selfish, narcissistic, or egocentric manipulators, but I will say that they may have some serious control issues, and may even be uncomfortable in their own skin. Jill and I make this personal, so we say it from the first person perspective. Because we recognize this fact, if we attempt to satisfy all the controllers in our daily experiences, then everyone will be happy, but us."

"Listen closely as I enunciate my personal philosophy on trying to satisfy other people at the expense of yourself. I cannot satisfy everyone and I will not try. If I try to satisfy everyone; everyone will be happy except me!"

"My." An enraptured Lizzy sighed. "That is powerful."

"But once we recognize what is happening, relative to talking about how we allow ourselves to be controlled by others, shouldn't it be simple enough for us to change the way that we think about the influences that we allow others to have over us? I mean couldn't we just cut the strings of control that are attached to us?" Asked Izzy.

"Izzy, those strings are long and deep and then deeper still. We have to go even deeper to appreciate the connectivity of the strings." Bill answered.

"Yes, I know, but couldn't we sever the strings at that deeper level that you are referring to?" Izzy further inquired.

WHO'S IN YOUR CIRCLES

CHAPTER THIRTEEN
Going Deeper to Understand the Strings

"Before I answer that," Bill queried. "Are you ready to go even deeper? And I mean that both figuratively and literally."

"Yes, sure." Both Izzy and Lizzy nodded approvingly.

"Well here we go." Bill continued. "Izzy you asked the question, couldn't we sever the strings at that deeper level? The truth is that the deeper level is the only place to cut them if it is going to be effective. However, it may not be as simple as one might think to cut the strings or resolve this issue, unless we understand that the source of many of our controlling thoughts, are actually below the conscious experience. I want you to think of your mind as an iceberg floating in a cold artic ocean. Most of the iceberg is below the water line and the little that we see is really only the tip of the iceberg."

"The conscious mind is represented by that small tip riding above the surface of the water. But the subconscious mind is the iceberg's massive mass, hidden just below the surface of the water. What I am saying is this, just about everything that we have learned in life, and many of the things that control who we are and how we see ourselves have their residence within the subconscious. And remember that most of the stuff that made it into our subconscious made it in when we were just children, before we were intelligent enough to filter or analyze the credibility of the information stored there. And what we have stored in our subconscious is the entire sum of what we have experienced in life; and I mean the good, the bad, and the ugly."

Jill interjected. "Our subconscious is the entire sum of our life experiences up to this moment. It has loads of input. Some of that input has been erroneous, harmful, and faulty. It is that input that has the greatest potential for steering awry with the illogical, unfounded, and groundless thoughts that we are not even aware of."

"Quite simply, to answer your question, most people cannot change the way they think, because they are not even aware of how they think or the possibility that they are in many instances no longer thinking. You see, their responses have become so automatic until they are disconnected from logical reasoning or the real thinking or cognitive process. It's like turning the steering wheel on a large ship. Though you might be turning the steering mechanism on deck, it is connected to a rudder down below the water level. It is that rudder that actually causes the ship to turn." Jill spoke in earnest.

Bill interjected. "With many people, they are no longer even attempting to steer the ship with the steering wheel. The vessel is running on a type of auto pilot. A pre-programmed script now turns the rudder. This is how many people make decisions without bona fide thinking involved at all. And even if the person, who is turning the wheel, gets conflicting responses from the ship, they simply revert to auto-pilot, because that is all that they know. There is no thought process exercised. There is no real thinking, because almost everything is accomplished by the pre-programmed scripts of the subconscious."

"They are responders to external stimuli with internal preset patterns of thought from the subconscious level that are not necessarily connected to logical thinking or reasoning. They operate in a sphere where they no longer realize that it is what's below the surface of the waters of the conscious level that is actually steering the ship or influencing and even controlling their decisions."

"These people continually deal with decision making in irrational and non-productive ways. They are very often stressed because the resolution of problems evades them, because they do not thoroughly employ thought. Instead they grab whatever pattern the subconscious

215

yields and try to make the problem fit their solution, rather than thinking of new solutions that truly address their problems." Bill concluded.

Jill continued Bill's line of thought. "One of the secrets in guarding your inner circles lies in understanding this critical concept. Otherwise those that come into your inner circles, who are on auto-pilot, may be extremely fixed in their thinking or lack thereof, with the concept that everyone is suppose to change and adapt to their view of the world. The constant demands that they will inevitably place on you and your relationship will forever be a source of tension and stress in your lives."

Buzz came the Q-Bugs, "Stress is air in the balloon called relationship. It can only take so much of this air before it pops. J. Calvin Alberty."

"They will not only continually bring stress into your life, but also into your relationships. These individuals, with their trunk full of inflexible thoughts would have you to think like them. They are insecure and very guarded in the presence of independent thinkers." Jill ended as Bill began.

"Their self-image, self-esteem, and motivation are all tied into their inflexible thought patterns. They will not and often times cannot change, because they are not willing to examine their beliefs on a deeper level. And it is only at this deeper level that permanent changes can take place. This is below the conscious-level or at the rudder-level. This is the very level at which the stored illogical and irrational thought patterns can and must be assaulted in order to effect permanent change in their lives."

"So as we reflect, we do not allow individuals into our inner most circles who do not think independently, and are at the command of generations of puppeteers pulling their strings. We also do not allow individuals into our inner circles who are having repeated problems. We do not do this because they are not dealing with the root cause of those problems at the rudder level. Instead they are wrestling with symptoms or steering wheels that are disconnected from the deeper thoughts at the rudder level. These deeper thoughts are the controls in charge of their auto-pilot. This is the same autopilot that controls and influences their behaviors."

WHO'S IN YOUR CIRCLES

CHAPTER FOURTEEN
Back To the Lands of Circles

The return trip from the Land of a Different Circle had left both Izzy and Lizzy exhausted. They both slept in late, but did meet as agreed upon in front of Lizzy's cottage at noon. The last thing that they had heard the Special Ones say was that they all may have to return to the Land of a Different Circle some time in the near future. They told them that only time could tell.

"Woe," Izzy smiled, alluding to their experience in the Land of a Different Circle. "That was an awful lot of information to think about wasn't it?"

"It certainly was." Lizzy laughed softly. "My head still hurts." She smiled as she rubbed her temples.

"Really?" A concerned Izzy responded.

"No, not really." Lizzy laughed again. "But it was really a lot of information to absorb in such a very short time period. And the most amazing thing about it is that I remember everything that happened there almost verbatim.

"So do I." A surprised Izzy replied. "I'm telling you Lizzy, I have seen the strangest things in this place, the strangest things."

They both laughed out loudly. They were happy because they knew that as strange as things were, they had learned so much and it was a comfort just being back in the Lands of Circles.

CHAPTER FIFTEEN
We All Start Out Winners

"I wonder what our next lesson will be about." Lizzy voiced as she pondered their future with the Special Ones.

"I don't know, but I am already excited at the thought of it, because I know whatever it is, you can bet that it will be interesting and informative." Izzy said thoughtfully.

"This really is a most amazing and intriguing place." Lizzy offered as she stared into the distant clearing.

"What are you looking at?" Izzy questioned as he began peering in the same direction. Before Lizzy could answer Izzy saw it too. It was a shimmering wind chime in the distance. They immediately knew that it was different, because this chime was fluctuating in colors and the sounds were not merely random noises that were driven by sporadic breezes. Instead, they were like symphonic melodies that repeated themselves in the exact same pattern each and every time.

They both moved in for a closer inspection. It was as if the pied piper called them forth like the children of Hamelin. They had to see and know more. There by the chime was an arrow. It pointed to another arrow, which pointed to another arrow, which they began following. They followed arrow after arrow until there were no arrows left to follow.

"What do you think it means?" Lizzy asked Izzy.

Izzy, with a curious smile, looked around and said, "I think it means that we're lost. We've been a lot of places, but we've never been here before."

"We're not lost." Lizzy assured him. "All we have to do is follow the arrows back in the reverse order."

"What arrows?" Izzy asked looking behind them.

"Those . . ." Lizzy stopped in the middle of her sentence. "All of the arrows are gone. I don't understand." A wide eyed disbelieving Lizzy verbalized.

"Remember where we are." Izzy whispered as he looked from side to side and all around. "Things might be strange here, but remember that everything that has occurred here has always had a purpose, even if not obvious at first. And something tells me that there is a purpose for our being here." Izzy words faded off as he began searching more earnestly around him for clues.

"There is something that we are to learn here, and I wonder what that something is?" Lizzy stated as she joined Izzy in investigating their surroundings.

"Lizzy!" Izzy called out as he discovered a large lake of shimmering clear water. There was a great deal of movement at the surface of the water. Lizzy was soon at his side gazing upon the lake's glassy, active, and reflective surface.

"What are they? Izzy asked Lizzy.

"They?" Lizzy responded.

"Yes, what are all of the things moving in the water?" Izzy asked trying to clarify his question.

"I don't know." Lizzy admitted.

"What does the sign say there beside you?" Izzy replied.

Lizzy looked at the sign that she had not noticed before, as Izzy pointed it out to her. Maybe she was too busy looking at the lake's shimmering surface that seemed almost alive. Or maybe it wasn't there before at all she thought as she began reading the sign. "It says, "Lake Genesis."

"Lake Genesis," Izzy slowly ran the name through his mind. "That's an odd name for a lake." Izzy voiced. "What are those little creatures moving near the surface of the water?"

"I don't know, but they look like tiny tadpoles, but I have never seen silver and chrome-like tadpoles. I've especially never seen tadpoles with light emanating from within them. And these tadpoles are so small." A confused Lizzy uttered.

"There must be millions and millions of them; perhaps billions, trillions, or even zillions would be more like it." Izzy muttered almost unable to believe his eyes. "Look, there's another arrow." He shouted. Again they were following arrows that led them completely around the lake and back to their original spot. They were exhausted. However, stranger than strange, when they got back to the original spot, it was totally different.

"How could this be? This is where we started, isn't it?" Izzy asked.

"Yes, but it doesn't look like it. Yet I am sure that this is exactly where we started." Lizzy hesitantly offered. "Look." She cried while pointing at a crystal clear box-like container beside the lake. Now I know for sure that this was not here before." She added.

"There is writing on it." Izzy said leaning closer to the box. "It says, we all start out here and we all start out as winners." They both paused, and were in deep and profound thought when Lizzy suggested, "Open the box."

When Izzy moved forward and began to do as requested by Lizzy, she could immediately see that there were several sheets of paper rolled into scrolls inside of it. Once Izzy had the box fully opened, they could see that there were three scrolls inside. Each had a single Greek letter on a wax seal that kept the scrolls intact. The first was the letter Phi. Lizzy unrolled it and began reading to Izzy. "Finding true understanding of your beginning is the genesis of finding yourself." She then opened the second scroll identified by the Greek letter Nu and began to read, "Newness of life begins with understanding your path, which you cannot understand without knowing your destination." Finally she reached in and pulled out the third scroll with the Greek letter Pi on it and began reading. "Pierce the darkness with light. You must influence the world so that your essence is bright, do not allow the world to darken you."

"I think that I know what it all means." Izzy smiled. "Genesis means beginning. We all began in the lake of life, right here. And we all began life as winners. There are as many as 300 million sperm cells in a single act of conception. Every one of them give their very all in the race of their lives and for their lives. They spend everything in their attempt to be first to make it to the egg and fertilize it, but only one does. Only one wins in this amazing race for life, a race for the genesis of a man or a woman. That means that every child that is born started out in life as a winner. They competed in a marathon against up to 300,000,000 other competitors and they won."

"I understand that Izzy, but what does this have to do with us allowing individuals into our inner circles?"

"Izzy if you don't mind, I will be happy to answer that." Jill offered as she and Bill approached.

"By all means, please." The surprised couple answered. Izzy and Lizzy were happy to know that a new and important lesson would now begin.

CHAPTER SIXTEEN
We Are Unique

The couples momentarily embraced in their happiness to see each other again. Jill immediately embarked upon her explanation, "Even though we all start out winners, the many encounters with life's challenging experiences have made too many people forget this very important fact. In their genesis they were great; and that greatness still resides in each of them. And even though they may have forgotten it, that greatness did not go anywhere."

"Listen," Bill interjected. "This is my part. I want you to think very deeply for a moment." Bill extended his hand with a small round object in it. "What do you see?" He asked.

"I see an acorn." Lizzy responded.

"And you, Izzy, what do you see?"

"An acorn." He responded.

"You're correct of course, on the surface it's just an acorn, but in reality it is so much more. When I look at it, I see a mighty oak tree. And beyond that I see the genesis of ten thousand forests."

Buzz came the sound of the Q-Bugs. "The creation of a thousand forests is in one acorn. Ralph Waldo Emerson. "

"And everything that this acorn ever needed to become those ten thousand forests was in it from the very beginning.

Buzz came the sound of the Q-Bugs once again.

"Everything that is needed,

Everything that is vital,

Everything that empowers,

Everything that pushes the oak tree toward the sky,

It was in the acorn from its very beginning. J. Calvin Alberty."

"Now think," Jill said. "If the universe would invest that type of power and intelligence in a simple acorn, how much more has it invested in its greatest creation, man?"

"The universe has called us into existence for a purpose!" Bill added. "We are not accidents. We are the product of the very mind of purpose. Realize that even each blade of grass has a purpose! So we must discover and live out the greater goals for our lives!"

Buzz came the sound of the Q-Bugs. "Great minds have purposes, others have wishes. Washington Irving"

"Listen closely." Bill intensified. "It is in discovering that purpose that we discover our greatness. In fact it is in finding our purpose in the Creator's will that will override all of the experiences that have served to negatively program us. Deep down inside each of us, even deeper than the strings of the puppeteers can reach, there is a pool of pain and hurt. However, above and greater than that reservoir, is an ocean of strength and courage. This is the source of that greatness which is our purpose."

Buzz came the sound of the Q-Bugs "Zig Ziglar said the opportunity for greatness doesn't knock; it's inside every one of us. However, we must work to get it out."

Buzz came another set of Q-Bugs, "Keep away from people who try to belittle your ambition. Small people always do that, but the really great make you feel that you too, can become great. Mark Twain"

Jill smiled warmly as she began. "You may ask yourself, what does this have to do with people entering your inner circles. Let me tell you in no uncertain terms, **EVERYTHING**. We cannot allow individuals inside our inner circles who do not recognize the greatness that is within them. If they do not realize their greatness, they will never strive for it. This is one of the greatest duties of all mankind, to strive to maximize the greatness within himself; and to give back to the universe by helping others to realize their own greatness and uniqueness."

"Yes along with this greatness is our uniqueness. There is a uniqueness about each of us that is second to nothing else created. It is prepared for each individual even before their conception, as Bill will explain."

"Answer this question." Bill laughed. "And it will not be about an acorn. How many people did it take to make you Izzy?"

"I don't understand." Izzy said after a brief pause.

"I mean how many people did it take to bring you into this world?"

"Oh I get it." Izzy responded, "Two."

"Exactly." Bill encouraged him toward the next question with confidence. "And how many did it take to make those two?"

"It took four, my two grandparents on my mother's side and my two grandparents on my father's side."

"And how many did it take to make the four?" He continued.

"Eight." Izzy answered.

"I think you're getting the picture, but let's review it one more time. How many individuals did it take to create those eight?"

"It took sixteen."

"Notice that the number of people keeps doubling. You begin with one then two, then four, eight, sixteen and so forth." Bill then showed Izzy and Lizzy the following chart.

WE BEGIN WITH YOU, ONE PERSON
THERE IS NO ONE ELSE LIKE YOU.
YOU ARE UNIQUE AND SPECIAL!
IN 12 GENERATIONS IT TOOK OVER
8,000 INDIVIDUALS TO MAKE A
VERY SPECIAL
1 =YOU
2
4
8
16
32
64
128
256
512
1024
2048
<u>4096</u>
8190

"There is no one else like you in the whole world!

And because you are unique and special, never compare yourself with others. Appreciate your own uniqueness. The universe has called you into existence. It has made you unique because there is something to be accomplished in the universe that you were made especially to do." Bill continued.

"In just 12 generations, it took over 8,000 people, compelled by their passions, love and for various other reasons, to come together to create that unique you. Do you understand the power of this statement?" Bill queried. "Understand that it took over 8,000 people in just twelve generations to bring the unique you into existence. No one else has the exact DNA, genetics or experiences that have made you who you are. You are a miracle. So be yourself! It is much better to be that distinctive you than a poor replication of someone else."

"Scream at the universe and say that people can accept me for who I am or reject me for who I am, but I am, who I am, and I am unique, running my own life toward my own unique destination."

Buzz came the sound of the Q-Bugs "When all think alike, no one is thinking very much. Walter Lippmann."

"If a man does not keep pace with his companions, perhaps it is because he hears a different drummer. Let him step to the music which he hears, however measured or far away. Henry Thoreau."

"We all have to get this point." Jill pressed. "Individuals who do not comprehend how important, how powerful, and how unique they are will be minions to mediocrity without ever having a real sense of direction or purpose. And if allowed in, they will infect your inner and outer circles with a poison for which there is no cure and a virus for which no remedy exist outside of those individuals themselves. And it is too much of a risk to wait for their awakening or for them to find their sense of direction and purpose. You may attempt to do this in your outer circles only if they are there for the specific reason of helping them, but you should never allow them into your inner circles."

"Again imagine yourself a large rechargeable battery as we spoke of earlier." Bill stated. "As that battery, remember that you only have so much life energy inside of you. Allowing these individuals or couples into your inner circles and having them continually draining the life and vitality from you, your life, and your relationships with your intimate other, is a sure formula for disaster."

"We have all heard the adage that we must "Do no harm" in a relationship, but many fail to see something that is at least just as important, and that is to be sure that we do not allow others to do harm to us. In light of this, we must understand that when we allow these individuals into our inner circles, that is exactly what we are doing, placing ourselves in harm's way."

"Please listen." Bill implored. "We are in no way saying give up on these individuals. They are important, and their lives matter greatly, but we are saying do not allow them into your inner circles in their present condition. They will drain you faster than you can recharge; and you will become vapid, insipid and effete."

Bill turned to Jill and asked her to tell them more about the acorn."

Izzy and Lizzy started to closely witness just how intimate Bill and Jill were. One could start a sentence and the other would finish it. "The acorn is amazing." Jill smiled. Though it has such great potential to become those 10,000 forests we spoke of earlier. There are four elements that it must have. Just as humans, in order to have healthy relationships, must have love, honesty, trust and respect; the acorn in order to grow, must have its four elements: soil, water, sun, and air.

"Here's the most important factor in what we are trying to say, you may be the soil, another person may be the air, still another may be the water and someone else the sun. Each may enter the person's life at different times or some at the same time. When water comes, it may not notice a difference in the acorn, but water still imparts its strength. At some future point, air comes and breathes oxygen, carbon dioxide, and nitrogen on the acorn and it also does not notice a change, but it still imparts its strength into the acorn. The sun shows up and sends it rays into the acorn, but it does not notice a change, but still it imparts and stores its solar strength into the acorn."

Jill continued, "Finally soil comes along and gives its strength to the acorn and the acorn with its reserves from water, air, and sun begins to rumble, shake, and burst forth to become the mighty oak which was its destiny from the very beginning. Then the soil declares, look what I have done. I have made the acorn into a mighty oak. The truth however, is vastly different; it was the strength of all four; as well as that strength which was in the acorn at its beginning."

Bill interjected, "We are telling you that when it comes to these individuals, give of your soul and your heart. You may be the rain, the wind, the soil or the sun. Whichever you are, there is one thing that you can be sure of, your giving will not return to you void. It will go forth and multiply itself a thousand times in people you have met and those that you have never met and will never meet. Your influence and energy will go forth and take on a life of its own. This is how our influence and energies operate in an intelligent universe."

Jill began, "The Great Creator is the author of all that is good and we are the channels through which His positive energy passes to others. But we are also the recipients of these forces as they pass to others. It continues to live after it departs from us and it possesses the amazing ability to alter lives for the better. However, until these lives are altered, they must not be allowed into your inner circles."

"What is this force called?" Asked Izzy.

"It has many names." Jill answered. "Some of the names by which it is widely known are: love, compassion, kindness, benevolence, helpfulness, sacrificing, altruism, philanthropy, empowerment, encouragement, inspiration, motivation, service and many others. And sometimes it has names like Uncle James, Big Mama, Gramps, mama, dad, and friend. However, they all correspond to the uplifting and empowering of the recipient."

Jill continued, "This force will always complete the Circle of Love and find its way back to you greatly multiplied. It is the nature of the

Circle of Love. In essence, love that is sent out will always find its way back home. It is sad to say that many people never receive love, because they never give love. That is why we must give love unconditionally."

"There will be many individuals, couples, and groups that will lack this vital component of love. If they do, even though they appear to have everything else, they truly have nothing. They are hollow and empty shells. This will be your next lesson. It will be a hard lesson, but one that must be learned. We must all visit a planet where love is rarely if ever seen."

"Personally, we hate going there, but it is a sacrifice that we make for our friends. It is imperative that you learn these truths that are to be revealed on the Planet Odium, which we sometime refer to as the Planet Loveless. It is urgent that you learn the lessons to be taught there, because at this very moment you are on the border of the Circle of Close Friendship with us. Therefore, it is imperative that you learn how to fully protect yourselves to the extent possible, because your pain, as close friends, will become our pain." With these words spoken, the Special Ones soon departed and Izzy and Lizzy were on their way home.

237

When Izzy and Lizzy returned to their cottages, they both had a small bronze sign fastened to their front doors. Each sign simply read "Remember the Acorn and the Circle of Love."

CHAPTER SEVENTEEN
The Dark Experience on the Planet Odium
AKA the Planet Loveless

The note from the Special Ones said, "Dress for a very cold environment. We will leave the Lands of Circles for another world filled with vastly different experiences and knowledge."

Izzy and Lizzy had serious consternations about the upcoming trip. The note had only heightened their anxiety and state of uneasiness. They were surprised to see, upon the arrival of the coach, the Special Ones were already aboard. They greeted one another with smiles and hugs. The carriage was quickly on its way.

"This coach is extremely well insulated." Bill informed Izzy and Lizzy. "Also notice that there is no coachman, nor is it being pulled by any creatures. Please understand that Jill and I have no control over this coach. We simply get on it the same way that you do and we can only observe what the universe has to teach in this cold and heartless region of darkness. The coach cannot be seen, heard, or sensed in anyway by those into whom environment it will enter." With that spoken, the coach was soon underway.

"Oh my." Lizzy said, referring to the sudden darkness and strange feelings of coldness.

"It's fine." Jill spoke in a calming manner. "My first experience to this place left me practically traumatized, but well informed. It will get very cold, that is why we asked you to dress warmly."

"Bill, didn't you say that the coach was very well insulated?" Izzy asked seeking confirmation.

"Yes." Bill answered. "But the temperature that we feel does not come from cold air in the surrounding atmosphere. That would be simple enough to deal with. This coldness is unique, for it is the result of the coldness of the hearts of those who inhabit the dark world to which we are traveling."

"We are here." Jill announced after a long trip through a realm of disquieting and gloomy darkness. The place was eerie to say the least. Izzy and Lizzy had been informed by the Special Ones that they would answer any questions they had on anything that they observed. However, Jill had stated that even they might not have the answers to everything in this dark and gloomy place.

"Instantly we will move from one scene to another." Jill began. "Usually it will be scenes of thematic importance. Simply put, we will witness different subjects related to the same theme. One theme will be presented and then another in quick succession. Pay very close attention to all that you see, because everything here, as it must in order to tolerate it, will pass relatively quickly. And by the way, this world is known by the name Planet Odium, which we also call the Planet Loveless."

"Look." Lizzy said soberly as she directed Izzy's attention through the large window of the coach. The scenes were horrific. There was hunger everywhere. Children were starving. Babies were crying in the arms of desperate mothers who had nothing left to give. This same scene was repeated with different cultures throughout the breadth of the planet.

The scenes quickly changed. Suddenly homeless people were everywhere. Just blocks from large multi-billion dollar companies, the poor languished in obscurity, penury and abject poverty. They were in alleys, under bridges, on the streets, and subways. They were cold, wet, sick and hungry. The wealthy considered them an inconvenience. They ordered their cardboard houses torn down. They were often mugged and the women raped, but little or nothing was done about it.

Again the theme changed. This time they were appalled to see the sick children. They were privy to the corporate books of large conglomerates that squashed cures that were natural and easily accessible. "Why would they do that?" Lizzy questioned through tear filled eyes.

"To quote The Book, The love of money is the root of all evil. These large corporations work with governmental agencies to pass laws that are all based on profit and increased revenues for their corporate officers and stock holders."

"They do this even while little children are dying?" Izzy asked.

"Yes." Answered Jill.

"But why do the citizens of this planet allow this to happen?" Izzy continued to question.

"They allow it to happen because of apathy, and because they have placed their faith in the heartless systems of this dark and frigid world."

"Well, why are the systems not working?" Izzy questioned still.

"Listen," Bill said softly, "There was a time on this planet when the governmental systems were for the people, of the people and by the people. It was a time when men and women served because they loved their countries. However, it is a vastly different world now. Elected officials serve themselves and the interests of a privileged few. Special interest group and lobbyists pay them huge sums of money to promote the interest of their companies rather than the interest of the people. And after they leave politics, they are very generously compensated with plush and cushy figurehead positions by the very companies and corporations, whose lobbyists pulled their strings while they were in office."

"But why do they give in to these companies and large organizations?" Lizzy pleaded for an answer that would help her understand how they could be so callous and cold.

"They are greedy." Bill replied. "They are greedy, greedy, greedy. They have enough financially to live on forever, but they always feel the need for more."

The scene then flashed to the unemployed with a digital type voice generated by the coach itself narrating the events in front of their eyes. They witnessed as million of unemployed men and women were fired from their jobs just before a celebrated holiday for children.

They saw large companies merged, down sized, and right sized with no loyalty to their employees. The citizens lost their homes, cars and other possessions due to no fault of their own, with the exception of trusting their greedy employers. They saw all of this happen while the companies amassed record-breaking profits for their stockholders.

The price of fuel skyrocketed to astronomical levels. The workers had to take their meager resources reserved for their children and desperate times to purchase the fuel that they could not live without. This occurred while gas companies realized record profits for the privileged few. Protest was unheard of as the masses knew that one or two months without their salaries would place them in the category of the homeless. They were all quiet about their fear of the very government that they had elected.

Izzy and Lizzy cried as did Jill. Bill was hurt so deeply that he could not cry. "Please take us away from here." Lizzy cried.

"We are not in control." Bill whispered.

A new theme came to the forefront. People were being discriminated against because their eyes were brown in color. They were denied access to housing, jobs and schools. The justice system created laws that targeted them and would make their lives miserable. With the words of a song in the background singing, "Keep *Your Eyes on the Prize*, Hold On;" some were hung as strange fruit on southern trees while crowds jeered and laughed. Others were brutally beaten.

Even young children were outfitted in garbs of hate by their twisted and sick parents who hated the brown eyes. The leader of the brown eyes was shot and murdered in the home of sweet Lorraine. It was the system's effort to destroy their dream for parity.

Again the scene suddenly switched. There were men and women making bombs, killing hundreds and thousands of innocent people in order to bring attention to their cause. They were crazed with hatred and ruled by intolerance. They sought weapons that could inflict greater and greater death and devastation. They loved no one, not even themselves. They did not see themselves connected to all humanity. They did not see that they were all the same. They did not see that they were one.

The behavior and ideology of the greedy and loveless had penetrated and perverted their minds to the point of insanity. They could not see that they were mere pawns in the hands of the greedy. It's like my grandmother often said, sometimes you can be at the circus so long that you cannot see the clowns. Therefore, they do not see that the clean hands of the greedy are never stained with the deeds of their evil.

Through psychological manipulation, financial gratification and finely orchestrated propaganda campaigns, the citizens were taught that it was unpatriotic to disagree with the rancid positions of the manipulated masses. Patriotism was the marching slogan of death used by the greedy to control the masses, as it was in the time of the mad man. Without examining their beliefs, the masses blindly rallied around them, even to their own demise. They voted for slick ad campaigns. They voted for 30 second glamour spots. They voted for what would protect their share.

They did not vote for what was good for the body humanity. They did not realize that the body humanity could only endure so much pain and that the pain could only be endured for so long before the whole body of humanity would rise up and rebel against its own self and die. It had the AIDS virus of hate. A diabolical virus that destroyed the body's only defense cells of love, respect, trust, and honesty; without which the whole body of humanity is doomed.

The scene changed again with a new theme. Prisons were crowded and over populated. "Why are there so many people incarcerated?" Asked Lizzy.

"Imprisonment is a business now. It is a new way to make money. Laws are enforced against the brown eyes and the have-nots with greater frequency and severity than against the haves. The law is reserved for those who can afford it rather than parity in the dispensation of justice."

"And what about the body of Lady Justice?" Asked Izzy.

Bill responded, "She is no longer blind. She sees silver, gold, and green against her own will. Lady Justice cries out in protest of the abuse imputed against her and her good name, but no one is listening to anything other than the ching-ching of greed and the greedy. Poor Lady Justice lies raped and prostrate on the bed of whoredom to be bought at a price against her will. She cries aloud, "That which is for sale was never meant to be sold!" She hates her position, but the greed of the greedy has bound her in her frailty to serve their sick and sadistic purpose."

However, upon a closer inspection; and with a more critical gander, the keen observer sees that the whore on the bed of abuse is not Lady Justice at all. It is her antithesis, the whore, Madam Injustice. And even she screams in protest that the price to be paid is too high and the consequences to be suffered too dire. But the band plays on for those who do not love truth. They dance the dance of delusion to a finality of horror and dreadfulness that is alas incomprehensible and even more-so inescapable.

"Will this ever end?" Izzy asked.

"Odium will continue to get worse and worse." Bill answered, "But one day the Great Creator of the universe will have taken all that He can and will step in and put an end to this darkness and the cold hearts of the greedy."

"The sad thing is this," Jill lamented. "The planet Odium was once called The Garden of Eden." With those words spoken, a deaf silence filled the coach as the awful and agonizing journey finally drew to a close.

As the coach made its way back to the Lands of Circles, Bill, still somewhat depressed spoke in a very sobering tone. "Those narcissistic, megalomaniacs residing at the top, and whose only goal is to secure more and more dollars for their coffers at the expense of humanity, must never be allowed into your inner circles."

"And those who aspire to be like these greedy tics that live by such despicable and shameful creeds as, "by any means necessary" and "only the strong survive" should never be allowed into your circles. Their coldness and lack of compassion, along with an appalling ruthlessness that is unparalleled, will one day not only destroy them, but you also, if you allow them into your circles."

"They are the sort of individuals that establish relationships based upon what they can get out of you and they are more interested in how you can promote their interests, rather than bonding based upon mutual interests, honesty, trust, love and respect."

WHO'S IN YOUR CIRCLES

CHAPTER EIGHTEEN
The Words of Wisdom

When Izzy and Lizzy returned to their cottages, there were two sheets of fine linen paper on top of the kitchen table in full view. Though each entered their own cottages, their eyes were immediately drawn to the papers. They both contained identical writings entitled "Wisdom."

WISDOM

Behold our house, the earth. Observe the family, of man. We are all the seed, of Adam. We are one. We have not made ourselves. Therefore, there is a Greater Power. He is the creator of all that is good and the sustainer of all that lives. Find your purpose in Him, for He is love. Come to know Him, for He is wisdom. Seek His path, it is truth.

See the world around you. In all of its complexity, it is yet simple. Go beyond the quaint huts by the side of the road and the over populated metropolis. See deeper than the abodes; they are only clay, straw, wood and mortar. Look deeper to observe the people. They are individual souls in search of joy and peace. They are the world. They are US. And the world can never be any worse or better

251

than the "you and I" in US. Therefore, we must strive to be ethical. Fairness must be much more than a philosophy. It must be a way of life. Look within yourself. If you look long enough and deep enough within, you will find a talent and a genius that is unique to you. And if you do not bring it to the table of brotherhood, we are all the lesser because of it.

Give generously of yourself. With diligence and determination, endeavor to improve the lot of those around you. Sow peace where there is turmoil, love amidst hatred, strength where there is weakness, and joy where there is sorrow. Give careful thought to your words before they are spoken. For your words have a power not fully comprehended. They can easily build or destroy a life. Let your utterances seek a path of humility. But ever remember, that silence continues to be virtuous. Speak your opinion quietly and rarely. For it is merely that, an opinion.

There are negatives all around you, if focused on; they will rob you of your energy and life force. They will steal your joy and leave you hopeless, avoid them. There are many positives, find them, laugh, for truly it is medicine for your soul.

Your body is a living temple, honor it with: clean water within and without, exercise, a wholesome diet of fruits nuts, grains and vegetables, sunshine in moderation, fresh air, meditation to the Living Creator, and a surrendering of all burdens to Him. Now, love yourself, knowing that you are of great value. For One much greater than us all thought enough of us to sacrifice everything on our behalf, far beyond our abilities to comprehend, appreciate, or empathize.

Be calm and do not become unduly disturbed by the affairs of this world. Remember, the world was here before you, and it will be here when you have long departed. It owes you nothing. Love not temporal things that you can not take with you beyond this veil of life. Instead love and develop indisputable character. Possess this character for yourself and in yourself. Bestow it through your words and actions to others. Accept people where they are, but do not be satisfied with their lack of growth.

Teach chiefly by precepts and examples, for many fools have spoken wisely, but their words have gone unheeded because they did not equate to their lifestyle. Your words will have a much greater influence when you do as you say or practice what you profess.

You were not born with a gavel in your hand. Nor do you possess infinite wisdom. You cannot read the hearts or motives of others. Therefore judge no one, for you have but one narrow perspective, that which is your own. Carefully put on the moccasins of others and walk lightly in their paths. Put on their glasses and see the world from their perspective. Implant within your bosom, their hearts, and feel their pain. I can assure you, the world will never be the same to you again. There remains a question that each person must answer of themselves and for themselves. "Is the world a better place as a result of my having been here?" Look long and pensively into the mirror, do you love the person you see? Evolve! Change! Become! And grow until you are in love with yourself.

There are no limits, boundaries or barriers that you cannot surpass if you dare to open your mind to the unlimited possibilities that are within you. Embrace your uniqueness. Look above you at the heavens in all of their celestial splendor, the stars, the moon, the planets, and the sun. Behold the vastness of this great and enormous universe. With all of its endless depth, breadth and height, there remains no room for odium, hate, ignorance and injustice.

Though we are many languages, many colors, and many cultures and ethnic diversities, still and always, we are one race--- HUMAN! And among humans, there is no beauty above love. And from love emanates forgiveness, tolerance, mercy, compassion, kindness and charity. Therefore, be beautiful, like the birds of spring speckled with colors of varying hues and filled with songs of promise. Be beautiful like the sun garbed in its robe of radiance as it sets beyond the endless sea. Be beautiful as citizens of the universe, a collage of colors and diverse nations that are bound by love and a common good for all.

We are billions upon the face of one earth! It is the household of humanity. A house divided against itself, cannot stand! There is but one earth. It cannot be divided. Therefore, we the people must love each other, and for those poor souls who have lost the capacity to love, as unfortunate as they are, at the very least, they must learn to tolerate the variances of others.

Whatever problem might confront the family of man, love remains the solution. Therefore, love the Creator, love yourself, love others and most definitely love life. For the day that you stop loving, you stop living.

THIS IS WISDOM!

Izzy and Lizzy were amazed at the writing and discussed its meaning in details. They both agreed that there was no greater power than love, and they further agreed that no one would ever enter their inner circles, who did not possess this wonderful power in copious quantities.

CHAPTER NINETEEN
The Universe and Confusion

Izzy and Lizzy were happy to see Bill and Jill on this beautiful and sun filled morning. They had expected them, according to their last conversation, at 7:30 AM. As usual, they were prompt and eager to embark upon teaching the lessons that this day would bring.

"Are you ready for our nature walk today?" Jill asked with a smile.

"We're as ready as ever." Izzy replied. They were soon deep within the forest. There they met a lady never seen before. Jill made the introductions. She introduced the lady as Mrs. El Hamilton, but she was affectionately known as Mrs. Hamilton, the mother of children on the Planet Sunset.

"Let me tell you just a little about Mrs. Hamilton." Jill began with a brief biographical sketch. "She was offered a great deal of money by the greedy to work for them. But she turned them down and chose to spend her life mentoring hundreds of children that were not her own. She taught them many principles that would help them to successfully maneuver their way through life. However, she also showed them how to have constructive fun while teaching them the

257

importance of adhering to rules. She taught them sports, games, hobbies, crafts, socialization skills and many other valuable lessons; but she is known mostly for her compassion, goodness, and love."

"She had the unique characteristic of believing that no child was disposable. She demonstrated this by giving her all toward every child's growth and development. Though most of the children that she served were poor and under privileged on the planet called Sunset; they were happy and their days were filled with fun. She treated every one of them as though they were her own."

"Today you shall see that her spirit is wonderful, her love is renowned and that she loves teaching. She is taking this time to teach you about the orderliness that must exist in all things if they are to be successful; even the order that must exist within your circles."

After a brief introduction by Bill and Jill, Mrs. Hamilton began. "This trip is not about a destination, but more so about the journey. In essence, we will learn whatever it is that nature has to offer us during the teachable moments presented to us today. She will work through you to let us know when the lessons are finished."

"Through us? How?" Lizzy's curiosity compelled her to ask.

"Trust the universe on this one." Mrs. Hamilton softly laughed. "Before this experience is over, nature will give you the answer to give to me."

"Ah, there's the first lesson taking place above in the trees." Mrs. Hamilton directed everyone's attention to a tree with a bird's nest resting on its branches. A mother bird was placing food in the mouths of the newly hatched birds occupying the nest.

"Of course we all know that baby birds are incapable of flying, but once hatched they need to eat. Nature has taken care of this by instilling within the parents an instinctual mechanism that drives them to go out and gather food for their young. However, still these young birds could not handle the great chunks of food that the parent birds gathered, so nature placed another mechanism in the birds so that they chew or grind the food up for their young nestlings so that it can be easily digested. This process does not only make the food easier to consume for the little ones, but by grinding the food beforehand, the adult birds have the ability to carry more food to feed their young."

"The point that nature is bringing forward through these birds is that nature has a sense of and a need for order. Without it the young birds would never survive."

"Again we find this lesson of order in the honey bees." Mrs. Hamilton smiled, "And bear in mind that you never have to be concerned or worried about studying these wonderful bees in the Lands of Circles; they do not sting. In fact they do not even have stingers. They fly to and fro gathering nectar from nearby flowers to carry back to the hive. After they make their superb honey, the bees in the hive consume it very sparingly. In fact, they communicate with one another on how far and in what direction the flower fields are from the hive."

"They then only take enough of the hive's resources to give them just enough energy to fly to the flower field and then return to the hive. They do not waste their resources because the food supply is very important to all of the inhabitants of the hive."

"This should be an important lesson for all life forms. Preserve not just for lean times, but to prevent lean times. These bees must at all times conduct themselves decently and in order if the hive is to survive. And similar hives that are on other worlds will quickly and efficiently deal with anything that poses a threat to its resources, because its resources are directly tied to their survival. But this is the Lands of Circles, where such behavior is not a problem."

"Consider the ants." Mrs. Hamilton further instructed while pointing to a mound near the roots of a large Magnolia-like tree. They gather all summer, spring, fall, and even in the winter, if the opportunity presents itself. Additionally they conserve what they gather, because they know that the winter will come. In their colony are soldiers, workers, and the queen. They all have their own areas of specific duties. If either group failed their task, the colony would not survive. All of their actions are purposeful and done decently and in order. Learning our purpose and role in life is indeed a monumental task."

"Take notice of the leaves on this plant. Have you ever noticed that they are not directly below one another, but instead are placed in a spiraling circular pattern around the branch of the plant? This allows for each leaf to have maximum exposure to the rays of the sun."

"If you watched each leaf over the course of a day, you would witness something that is very rarely observed because the process is so slow. Each leaf rotates with the movement of the sun so that its rays are fully exposed to it. Watch closely and you will observe how some flowers trace the steps of the sun across the sky. This is the type of order which is inherent in nature and is designed in all of creation."

The lessons, which all dealt with the orderliness of nature, went on for the better part of the morning and toward the evening. It was Lizzy who said, "I hate to say it, but I am getting tired."

Mrs. Hamilton replied while smiling at Lizzy, "I told you that nature would let us know when her lessons were finished through you. There is a major lesson that you should have learned from what you have witnessed today."

"The forces of the universe, however small or large that universe might be, demand order. They will not and cannot release their creative and restorative powers to the authors or nurturers of confusion and chaos."

"Therefore, in relationships, you must not allow individuals into your inner circles that stir up or foment confusion. This could be in how they communicate, their deeds, or whatever avenues they choose. Your circles must be free of these types. These are your circles; you not only have a right, but a duty to keep out all who would disturb the harmony and order that should exist within them."

Buzz came the Q-Bugs, "Associate yourself with people of good quality, for it is better to be alone than in bad company. Booker T. Washington."

"These people are everywhere. They will tell lies with tidbits of truth attached to them, or truth with tidbits of lies attached to them in an effort to create controversy and confusion. They will expose very personal things about you that they know can be damaging. Their loyalty is only to themselves. They are sycophants and panderers to those who are in positions to elevate them. They will sell their souls to the forces of darkness for a moment of fame and praise."

"Not only should you keep them out of your inner circles, but you should not converse with these sorts for they will twist your words like the tendrils of a vine. They disturb the order and tranquility of life because their esteem is low and they desperately desire attention. They do not care if that attention is negative or positive as long as it is attention. They desire this attention more than they value friendship." Mrs. Hamilton continued.

"Observe them at a distance, monitor their sinister behavior, and examine their dastardly motives, but do not allow them into any of your circles, and if these types are in the circles of would-be-friends, you must keep those would-be-friends out until they have purged them from their circles. They are dangerous!" Were Mrs. Hamilton's final words. With that said, Izzy and Lizzy were immediately back at their cottages.

"Wow, we're home." A surprised Izzy declared. "Did you hear that Lizzy?"

"Did I ever." She responded. "You even have to know what types of people your would-be-friends are associating with."

"If you do not, it can be perilous." They both repeated.

"This is much more than a simple matter of convenience or having order in our relationships. We should keep those who cause confusion out of all of our circles for a much more important reason." Izzy stated.

"I know." Lizzy replied.

"We must keep them out because of their destructive nature!" They both exclaimed.

Lizzy acted as if she had just experienced a sudden epiphany. "Wow! We really are home." Lizzy said seeming to have just comprehended her surrounding. "Things happen so quickly here." She said as they both simultaneously burst into laughter. Their time

264

in the Lands of Circles was often filled with learning and growth oriented experiences. Therefore, they had come to cherish their private and personal time together."

"Again they knew that they had learned more about establishing strong relationships by adhering to the rules of the circles. They both vowed to hold the rules and guidelines of the circles as sacred. They knew that one of their primary goals in life was to have a relationship that would be conducive to growing love and sowing peace. They were surer now than ever before that they were finding their way to their path of peace, order, love, and oneness. And the beauty of it all was that they were discovering and finding it together.

WHO'S IN YOUR CIRCLES

CHAPTER TWENTY
Another Lesson in the Path

It had been quite awhile since the Info-Bugs had been seen by Izzy and Lizzy. They had resolved between themselves that they needed to solve as many problems as they could on their own. However on this day, or should I say night, Izzy and Lizzy walked out of their separate doors to be presented with one of the most beautiful light spectacles ever witnessed. The Info-Bugs were hovering, flying and zooming back and forth to create the most indescribable light show in the air.

"It is so beautiful, but what does it mean?" Lizzy asked an Izzy, who was just as clueless of the purpose of the light show as was she.

"I wish I knew." An honest Izzy confessed while enjoying the wonders and sensations of this most beautiful festival of lights.

"Let's ask the Info-Bugs." Izzy suggested.

"Info-Bugs at you service."

"It's been a long time." One of the now familiar Info-Bugs broadly smiled with his sparkling white teeth. Afterward, they all smiled to reveal their own beautiful white teeth. Izzy and Lizzy wondered how was it that they all now had teeth, but neither asked the question.

"What is your name?" Lizzy asked the familiar Info-Bug."

"My name?" Izzy and Lizzy could see that he was caught off guard by the question, and after a brief pause he smiled even brighter. "My name is Harry."

"My name is Whiskers." Another offered.

"My name is Diamond." A more feminine voice chimed in. Suddenly, there was a barrage of names being broadcast by the Info-Bugs:

"My name is Pinky"

"My name is Baby Blue"

"My name is Winky"

"My name is Sweetie"

"My name is Ginny Pig"

"My name is Bouncy"

"My name is Snewdie"

"My name is Joker"

"My name is Snoozy"

"My name is Nosie"

"My name is Rosie"

"My name is Whimp"

"My name is Feisty"

"My name is Stanka"

"My name is Joon Poon"

"My name is Foots"

"My name is Bucky"

"My name is Bow Legs"

"My name is Charlie Bell"

"My name is Big Rick"

"My name is Grampie"

"My name is Buster"

"My name is Mel-Chapell"

"My name is Antzy"

"Enough!" One of the Info-Bugs politely yelled. "The rest of you can introduce yourselves on our next visit.

"We are so pleased to see you all again." Lizzy responded.

"And it is nice to meet some of your for the first time." Izzy added.

"You have been so very helpful to us, and we just don't know how we could have made it without your most needed and valuable assistance." Lizzy affirmed expressing their gratitude.

"It has been our pleasure." Harry replied with his scratchy little voice.

"Indeed, indeed." Diamond agreed, "But why haven't you called on us as frequently as you had in the past? We missed you."

"You do like us don't you?" Whiskers asked.

"Well of course we do." Izzy and Lizzy stated emphatically.

"It's just that we wanted to be more independent and find our own solutions. We know that when we go back into our own world we will not have access to you." Lizzy began. "I mean we would love to take you all with us if it were possible."

"More than you could ever know." Izzy echoed respectfully.

"I see." Harry smiled. "We understand, but at least you can call us to socialize with on rare occasions before you leave the Lands of Circles."

"We can?" Izzy questioned.

"While sure you can." Whiskers encouraged.

"We really like you. And we cannot say that for most of the people that we've met. Most were so dreadful that they never made it pass the Land of Associates." An emotional Diamond said. "But we like you guys."

"Oh we like you too. We would have spent more time with you earlier, but we thought that you were too busy. I mean, we've never seen you socialize, not even with each other. It seems that you are always working." Izzy responded.

"We are." Harry agreed, "But we're not too busy for you. You're close friends now."

"What do you mean close friends?" Lizzy quickly inquired, while almost bursting with excitement.

"Look at your wrists." Harry laughed.

"Yeah, look around your wrists." Diamond added.

"But Bill and Jill never said a word." Lizzy smiled at Izzy with tears in her eyes.

"It's not something that you have to say or talk about." Harry broadly smiled.

"It's something that you know." Whiskers laughed softly.

"It's down in your soul and you know it with every pitter-pattering beat of your hearts." A teary Diamond smiled broadly.

"Why do you think we're all lit up in the night sky?" Harry asked.

"Is it because of us?" Izzy and Lizzy questioned innocently.

"Why don't you ask the Special Ones?" Harry hinted with a wink and a smile.

"Yeah, why don't you ask us?" Bill and Jill repeated Harry's question as they walked up behind Izzy and Lizzy.

They had a group hug that was full of tears, warmth and love as the Info-Bug enveloped them. With the exception of Harry, Whiskers, and Diamond, all of the Info-Bugs exploded heavenward, while emitting a more intense and brilliant light display than ever before. The sky was inundated with an explosion of colors and radiance that grew brighter and brighter in intensity. Harry, Whiskers, and Diamond quickly joined in on the miracle in the sky. It was a celebration that lasted for what seemed like forever.

Never was there a single moment that was absent of ecstasy. Izzy and Lizzy were smitten and consumed by the amazing kaleidoscope of colors dancing across the sky.

The next day got off to a strange start. When Izzy and Lizzy awoke, they immediately noticed that they were no longer in little cottages, but very large and spacious homes. Fortunately, they were still next door to one another as they discovered when they walked outside. It was a whole new land. It was beautiful and it exuded with tranquility.

In the midst of their discovery, Izzy and Lizzy suddenly remembered that they had a noon appointment with the Special Ones. Izzy and Lizzy were not only aware of their newly acquired surroundings and their new status as close friends, but they were even more so aware of the responsibility that came with their close friend status.

"So glad to see you, come in." Jill directed them to the table.

"Here's a new rule." Bill asserted as he pointed to the books that had been opened prior to their arrival and placed on the table. "Almost every close friend has another close friend." Bill stated and then waited for their responses.

"What do you think about Bill's statement?" Jill asked after neither Izzy nor Lizzy verbally responded.

"I think that it means that everyone has their own set of circles?" Izzy offered after pondering Bill's statement.

"That's part of it." Bill continued, "But only a part. As close friends, we may at times share with one another things that we do not want anyone else to know. We will share these sensitive bits of information for many reasons such as seeking a more objective viewpoint to something that we might have under consideration."

"Because we respect you, we also respect your opinions and views. It doesn't mean that we are obligated to accept those views as a panacea or a cure-all. In fact we might ignore them completely. But hopefully, we will gain better insight to help us solve whatever it is that we are attempting to figure out." Bill stated.

"But here's the other side of that coin. Almost everyone has what is called a best friend. And that best friend might have a best friend as well. And that best friend might have another best friend. At any rate, when you share something with a close friend, or a close friend shares something with you, you must always remember that your close friend circle is unique to you and that specific close friend. The information in that specific close friend circle must never be shared with any other close friend in any other close friend circle; ever!"

"Once you share a confidential statement outside of that specific circle, it is no longer confidential." Bill added. "It is the beginning of the demise of that circle of closeness."

"A whispering campaign is begun, and those who are whispering will never give you the benefit of the doubt. Each time it is whispered, it will worsen. It may eventually find its way back to you, but the damage done is often irreversible." Bill concluded.

"You don't chase down rumors. That will only make them worse. It is also a sign of insecurity. If you hold the rules of the circles sacred, you will quickly know through whom the information originated or started. It is then time to move that person or couple outside of all of your circles. It is not something that you think about or contemplate. It is simply something you do. And you do it immediately. If they can ever make their way back into some of your outer circles, you must never make yourself vulnerable to them again. Know that if you do, you do so at your own peril." Jill verbalized in a very definitive manner.

WHO'S IN YOUR CIRCLES

CHAPTER TWENTY-ONE
It Did Not Start Out that Way

Izzy and Lizzy had recently been conversing with the Info-Bugs on a regular basis. It wasn't always to ask questions, but in response to the Info-Bugs' request to socialize with them. They enjoyed the Info-Bugs' company, and beside they were smart, funny, and entertaining.

"See ya." Harry said right before he, Whiskers, and Diamond disappeared. Izzy and Lizzy had a question for the Special Ones. It was related to something that Jill had mentioned one evening sometime earlier. As they walked through the garden of roses they had an unplanned, but fortuitous encounter with Bill and Jill.

"You are just who we wanted to see." Lizzy expressed after heartfelt salutations had been duly rendered. "I have two questions if you have the time to answer them."

"We'll do our best." Jill assured.

"How many more Lands of Circles are there?"

"There are three more Lands of Circles that are beyond the Land of Close Friends." Jill answered.

"The first is the Land of Intimates." Bill interjected.

"The next is the Land of Intimate-of-Intimates. The third is called the Land of Intimate-Self." Jill put forward with a sense of sacredness. "These are lands that are very, very rarely traveled, and almost never by more than two travelers at a time. We will be happy to tell you more about these lands later. What was your second question?" Jill petitioned.

"The second question is related to something that Jill said. On a more personal level it really caught my attention." Lizzy confessed. "I have frequently thought about it, but I am still not quite clear on it."

"Perhaps I can bring clarity to you, what did I say that was so perplexing?"

"You said that in a healthy relationship, your spouse should be the closest person to you. I think the world of Izzy, but we have only dated a year. I love him with all my heart, but I still feel very close to my mother and father. They have always been there for me and we have come through some very difficult times; times filled with sickness, financial stress, loss of love ones, and just some very personal defining moments. And they have loved me even when I did not deserve their love."

"When I was sick they spent everything they had and even went into serious debt to restore my health. When I wanted to attend the best fashion design college, they sacrificed again, because it was renowned for its famous graduates. They took out a second mortgage on their home to help finance that education. Does that mean that Izzy and I, or shall I say our relationship is unhealthy?"

"No, not at all. My mother was the same way with her mother and father. I was the same way with my mother. My father passed when I was still a young child. During the time when Bill and I first met, we were both very close to our parents. I guess you can say that when it comes to our very special relationship, it did not start out that way."

Bill softly took Jill by the hand and she knew that he wanted to tell their story in his own words. After she nodded approval, he asked her softly. "Then you don't mind?"

"Not at all, in fact, I kind of enjoy listening to you recount the events." Jill disclosed.

"Our meeting was a miracle in itself." Bill began. "I attended a small southern college affectionately known at the time as The College by the Sea. My line brothers and I had just crossed the burning sands, or made the Gamma Chi Chapter of our illustrious and noble fraternity. It was customary to take a road trip and meet the brothers on other campuses throughout the South. There were three of us traveling together; Cream, Zeus, and myself. We arrived at another State College around midday after leaving our campus early that morning. We immediately bonded with a few of the fraternity brothers who resided there. I remember Big Bell, Michael and some others."

"They quickly planned a little welcome party at the fraternity house for us. We had only one problem, we didn't know any young ladies there. It was now early evening, about 7:00 PM when we entered the student union building. Upon entering, immediately across the room, at a distance I saw this beautiful sweet country girl by the name of Jill Harper. Her friends called her Abby. I did not have a clue as to who she was at all. But I tell you from my heart, the very moment that I first laid eyes on her, and I know that this sounds crazy, but somehow I knew that she was that special lady for me."

"Now, when I say that special one, you have to consider, when I was 14 and my oldest brother was 15, he informed me that he would not get married until he turned 80 years of age. I quickly responded to him with a conviction beyond this world, that I would get married a year after him. So marriage was the furthest thing from my mind. Yet, here I was gazing at Jill for the very first time as if I had known her my entire life. I knew beyond a shadow of a doubt that this very beautiful young lady was the one with whom I wanted to spend the rest of my life and beyond." Bill stated emphatically.

"I turned toward Zeus and simply said I am going to marry that girl."

"How did you know?" Lizzy asked in a very soft voice.

"I don't know." Bill said thoughtfully. "Maybe it was simply infatuation, but whatever it was initially, there was something amazing about her smile. Oh my goodness, when she smiled, the whole room lit up. It wasn't just her mouth that smiled. It seemed as if her whole face smiled."

"I quickly directed Cream's and Zeus' attention to her and asked if they knew her. Cream said that he knew her sister. I don't know where I got the boldness from, because I was somewhat timid when it came to approaching young ladies. However, on that evening I was more afraid of missing an opportunity of a lifetime. Something cried out within me, go forward or live your life with regrets. I asked Cream to introduce me to her and he did."

"After a brief introduction, I told Jill and the other two young ladies with her, that we were in town for just one day and that we were wondering if they could join us at a small social gathering at the fraternity house later that evening. They said that they would think about it, but for the moment they were more interested in looking for a ride to get something to eat."

"I would find out later that Jill almost never went to the student union building at night. This was possibly her second or third time since attending college. She had missed dinner in the dining hall and was really hungry. So when her friends came by her room and made the suggestion that they should try and find a ride to get something to eat, she readily agreed."

"I volunteered to give them a ride though I did not even have a driver's license or a car. In fact, I had traveled there as a passenger in Cream's car. We stopped at a local fast-food restaurant. Jill ordered food, but I was so infatuated and lovesick that I honestly did not have an appetite at all. I was totally smitten for the first time in my life by the love bug. So I just sat there and watched her eat her fries, soda, and hotdog."

"Do you really remember those kinds of details?" A curious Lizzy asked.

"Yes very clearly. Jill wore a pair of bell-bottom jeans with a pull-over blue top that had one yellow and one orange sleeve with thin orange strips of material on the sleeves. She wore a denim cap with a wrap-around brim on it. She had a pair of wired-rimmed granny glasses, and on her jeans was a miniature turtle-like patch with the phrase, don't rush me. She also wore a pair of low-cut dark brown suede shoes. Listen I remember everything about that night, even how she smelled." Bill reminisced.

"Even how she smelled?" Lizzy leaned in closer.

"Yes, she smelled clean, like a fresh bar of soap. I guess that she had taken her shower and was in for the night when her friends came by. The three of them did join us at the modest gathering that night. We danced to a few songs and then exited to sit on the front porch of the frat-house. It was there that we talked, listened, and then talked some more."

"Mostly our conversation was about what we wanted to do for the future. I was mesmerized by her every word. There was a song that I heard that night for the very first time. It was entitled *"Lean on Me."* I took the occasion to lean my head onto her shoulder. It was amazing. The night ended far too quickly. When we dropped the young ladies off at their dorm, I got Jill's address and vowed to write her."

"I wrote about 120 letters expressing my love for her. Jill almost never wrote back. It was really hard trying to get her attention, but with every letter I tried to let her look deeper into my soul. I felt that if she knew me better, she would fall in love with me. I did not know that after she read my letters, she kept them for a few days and tossed them away."

"Though I had enlisted into the Air Force, my enlistment was on the delayed enlistment program. This meant that I was given ninety days to finish that quarter of school before I had to report for duty. Finally, as my time drew to a close and no responses were forthcoming from Jill, I decided to write my last letter to her. Part of it went something like this."

"In the universe there are things that are meant to be. Things like breathing to live; the sun and light; stars in the sky; colors in rainbows and butterflies; wetness in water; heat in fire, cold in ice, and you with me. I know the difference between chance and fate. I sense in my innermost essence; in the pith and very depth of my soul, that our meeting was fate. It was our destiny, and a providence that was inevitable and inescapable."

"I can rest now, because I know that the universe is now complete. For on that night, time paused. It stood still in respect for the moment that I first set eyes on you. Now the universe in all of its splendor and majestic intelligence has in its own way acknowledged that we were called into existence for such an occasion as THAT NIGHT; when we faithfully kept an unknown, but divine appointment on the calendar of love. You are the four elements of breath that have brought life, purpose, meaning, and substance to one who was indifferent, detached, aloof, and apathetic. We are, with a pureness and certainty meant to be together."

"Yet I regrettably realize that one man's view of the world is only one man's view. I cannot persuade you to love me if you do not. Though I am so in love with you, it is a love unrequited. I have been driving down a one way street lined with stop signs and flashing red stop lights on every corner. They were there all along, but I refused to see them and stop in my pursuit of your love, because to do so meant facing the very harsh reality of having to live life without you."

"I will not write you again. I know now that respecting you and loving you means loving you enough to let you go. But how can I let you go when I never really had you. Please forgive me if I have in any way troubled you, even for one unnecessary second with my hopes, dreams, and desires of winning your love."

"Be at peace knowing that one day, if you so desire, you will make someone the happiest man alive. I am only saddened that I am not that man. I must finally accept the reality that I have too long evaded; not being that special someone for you. So If I receive no response from this final letter, as much as it pains me, I will never disturb you again with my futile and ineffectual romantic efforts. Though I have told myself over and over that you do not love me as I do you, please charge it to my heart. You see, my heart, it hasn't heard you yet. It does not yet know to stop loving you, and I do not think that it will ever know how. Signed, alone and lonely, Bill."

"Wow, what did you do with a letter like that Jill?" It was Izzy this time with the question.

"Well on this occasion, while I read the letter, an associate of mine was there with me. I don't know why, but I read it aloud in the room with her listening. Maybe I wanted to get her opinion. When I finished, you could hear a pin drop. My friend-girl stared at me as if she was waiting for the next shoe to fall."

"Are you going to write him?" She finally had the courage to ask.

"I don't know." I answered.

"Well let me know what you decide." She insisted.

"When I asked why, almost without hesitation she said, if you are not going to write him, I am."

"Did you write him?" Lizzy quickly questioned.

"Believe it or not, I called him." Jill smiled.

"It was the happiest day of my life." Bill interjected passionately. I was on cloud nine for a solid month; who knows, maybe cloud ten. We met on several occasions for very brief periods before I began my tour of duty in the military. I had asked Jill to marry me and she accepted. I am telling you all of this to make a point. Our relationship did not start out with Jill in my intimate-of intimate circle. That position is not something instantly or easily acquired."

"I probably wrote Jill another hundred letters while I was in the Air Force. Basic training was a very difficult and lonely time. I finally asked her father for her hand in marriage. He just laughed and asked if I could feed her. This was his way of asking if I could support her. With confidence, I told him that I could and on August 17, a Friday evening, we were married in Denver Colorado. We were both far away from our families. It was just the two of us. We only had six people at our wedding. And one was Jill's maid-of-honor, which she met at the apartment's mailboxes the day before the wedding."

"The Chaplain's name was Pastor Hansen. He told us that no matter what happened in our relationship; never go to sleep angry or upset with one another. And for all the years that we have been married we have honored those words."

"Now listen, because I am about to tell you how Jill moved into my intimate-of-intimate circle. First it was the immense love that I knew that she eventually possessed for me and that I held for her from the very start. She gave birth to our three sons, which deepened our love. And I was actually able to watch the miracle of birth two of those three times. On another occasion, for eight days, we held hands and prayed, not knowing if our youngest son was going to live or die. We had the prayers of others and divine intervention by God. We grew closer and closer through these ordeals. I was diagnosed with cancer. After surgery, radiation therapy and the awful sickness that went with it all, it was Jill's love and support that was the foundation of life for me."

"Our middle son was then diagnosed with a strange type of cancer. It was a type of cancer that essentially attacked young children. We watched him grow weaker and weaker. The doctors said that they could not do anything for him. We then went to naturalists and herbalists. We believe that it was God working through them that cured our son."

"This experience brought us even closer. Our oldest son had to have a cornea transplant in order to retain his sight. These are only a few of the experiences that we, Jill and I had that placed us deeper into each others' inner most circles. We call these the defining moments that moved us closer to each others' inner most circles."

"Wow, I am sure that these experiences built your inner-circles up for Jill, but what event most brought Bill into your inner circles Jill?" Izzy questioned.

Jill became excited as she began to answer. "I know that we are talking about defining moments for moving into these inner most circles, but remember that it is the fullness of the life as well. All of the things that Bill enumerated helped him to move into my inner most circles."

"Maybe I can answer your question with this particular event. One day I was on the gurney being rolled into the operating room for surgery. Two doctors had determined that I had bone cancer and now all that was needed was the biopsy to give the final confirmation. While I was in the hall lying on the gurney on my way to the operating room and prepared to go into surgery for that biopsy, Bill placed his hands on my leg where the biopsy was to be performed. He then prayed; and I distinctly remember him saying, God if my wife has cancer, please take it from her right now and give it to me. Lord I ask you this with all of my heart, please take her cancer and give it to me."

"Two things soon followed that experience. I was found to be free of cancer and a month or two later, Bill was diagnosed with cancer. We do not know if his prayer had anything to do with it, but that is the type of love that brings one into the inner most circles. Like I said, we cannot say that Bill actually received my cancer, but my, my, what an amazing coincidence. And the truth is, because Bill could love me enough to pray a prayer like that, my inner circles were wide open to him."

"A new relationship doesn't necessarily start out with your mate being in your Intimate-of-Intimate Circle. It may take time, but if your relationship is healthy, your intimate partner or spouse will eventually inhabit that very special Intimate-of-Intimate Circle." Jill concluded.

"I lost my grandmother who was everything dear to me. And Jill lost her mother." Bill explained. "We both lost a brother each. But through it all, we grew closer together, and through our trials our love for each other increased."

"Don't get me wrong, there were great times also; like meeting the Scotts in Alamogordo, NM. They had the most wonderful relationship of any couple that we had ever known to this date. They were very special mentors for us. They even adopted us, not legally, but lovingly as their children. Even though Papa Scott has passed on, this very day, we still call them our other parents."

"All of our boys finished high school and attended college. One has acquired an advanced degree. Another has received a terminal degree. The youngest will soon graduate with his undergraduate degree. The oldest married a sweet young lady and they have given us two beautiful grandsons."

"Through it all we fall asleep each night in each other's arms. If you ask me what are some of the things that have sustained us, I would have to say that sometimes it was just the silence of our quiet times together. It has also been our words, our tears, our prayers, our touches, and our love for each other that has comforted us. However, more than everything else, it has been our knowledge of and our relationship with God that has brought us the greatest comfort."

"This is what has helped us in understanding and mutually accepting situations that we knew that we were powerless to change or do anything about. You see, through it all we had two things that kept us through the dark storms of life; the main support was God, and second only to Him, we've had each other. And that is how a relationship is built where your spouse is your closest and most Intimate-of-Intimate Friend. It doesn't just happen. It takes commitment, respect, love, trust, honesty, and a simple desire for the other person to realize their fullest potential."

"Oh, you may accidentally hurt one another on rare occasions, but you never purposely hurt each other. So when the other person makes a mistake, you can be comforted that it was truly a mistake, because you know deep down inside that they would never do anything to purposely interfere with your happiness, or steal your joy, not even the joy of one moment."

"Keep this concept ever before you, because time is precious. Remember these two truths: that real time is like the unstoppable flowing of sand through an hour glass that can never be turned over; and there is only so much sand left before time expires. Therefore, knowing that our time is limited, we must strive to find the happiness of each day. This is the second truth. We are responsible for our own happiness. We must not only accept, but embrace the responsibility for our own happiness! After all, happiness is a choice."

The session ended with these final words of wisdom, and once again Izzy and Lizzy experienced the much sought after growth inside their own inner circles.

CHAPTER TWENTY-TWO
Prelude to a Dark Activity That Must Never Enter Any Circle

"I have a question." Izzy announced to Jill and Bill. "In our world outside of the Lands of Circles, there are those who really don't have the commitment, respect, love, trust, and honesty for their spouses. I do not say this in judgment, but as the result of my observations. I cannot bring myself to even call these individuals intimates, because true intimates will not commit these very gross acts against other intimates as do these people."

"This is true." Lizzy joined in. "Society labels it as domestic violence. It is a horrible situation for not only a spouse to have to go through, but also many of these people have children who live their lives in absolute fear, not knowing what the next moment might bring."

"We are acutely aware of domestic violence." Jill replied to a surprised Izzy and Lizzy.

"You are?" Lizzy asked.

"Yes we are." Bill stated in a very sobering tone. It is something I guess we should talk about more, but we just don't have those types of individuals in our inner or outer circles. And it is not as though we have purposely ostracized them, we just honestly have never even associated with anyone like that; at least not to our personal knowledge."

"We visited the Planet of Dark Circles and we learned a great deal about it there. Bill and I even wrote dissertations on domestic violence. It was our goal to study it and help those who might be involved in it."

"I have a great idea. Why not take a journey to the Planet of Dark Circles right now. The journey is only a few minutes in the space coach." Jill suggested.

After they all agreed, a few seconds later the space coach appeared. It was the same coach that had taken them to the Planet Odium. Izzy remembered that the coach was extremely well insulated. It had no coachman, nor was it being pulled or drawn by any creatures. And if Izzy was correct in his thinking, no one controlled this coach. It had an intelligence of its own. It could not be seen, heard or sensed in anyway by those living in the environment in which it entered.

"Any questions before we depart?" Jill asked.

"Yes, the last time we were aboard this coach, you asked us to dress for a cold environment. Do we need to change clothes for this trip?" Lizzy asked.

"That's an excellent question." Jill smiled, but the truth is stranger than fiction. The environment in this place is so cold, that the coach must completely insulate us. You will not sense any of the foul coldness that exists there."

"One other question," Lizzy continued. "You call this the Planet of Dark Circles. Why is so much of what we experience in these different places referred to as circles?"

CHAPTER TWENTY-THREE
A Quick Lesson on Circles

"We will allow the coach to get underway while we explain the phenomenon of circles." Jill said as she pressed a button. "Pressing the start button is the only part that we have in controlling the coach. Everything else is on automatic." After a brief pause Jill continued. "You will discover that circles are everywhere. From the largest to the smallest structures that we are aware of, circles are involved."

"The galaxies and the universe is a circle. The minutest atom is a circle. Almost everything that happens around us is connected to circles. Rain falls; it supports animal and plant life. The sun draws it back up to the atmospheric heaven where it forms clouds. The clouds then give rain again and the circle continues."

"Listen." Bill began. Even in something as essential as life support systems we can find the circle. For instance, we live in an environment where we breathe oxygen. After taking the oxygen in, we then give off carbon dioxide. The plants around us will then make use of the carbon dioxide that we give off. Those very same plants now give off oxygen for us to use and the circle continues."

Jill began and continued without a pause. "Even the seasons move in a circle. You have spring, summer, fall and winter. The circle then repeats itself over and over. The sun rises then sets. All of this occurs because the planets themselves move in circles."

"When it comes to reproduction," Bill reflected. "And two people come together; an egg and sperm cell unite. An embryo develops into a fetus. Then an infant is born. The infant becomes a toddler, which grows to become a young child. The child moves into adolescence and then into young adulthood. In this stage he or she usually meet someone of the opposite sex and falls in love. They date and then are engaged. They get married and if they desire, they produce children of their own. They move into late adulthood and then they achieve senior citizen status and they live out their lives as actively as possible and eventually they pass on. Their children repeat this circle and then their grand children and so forth. It's all about circles."

"There are other circles that are not so noticeable." Bill started in. "If we sow bad seeds, we can be sure that we will reap the harvest from those seeds. If we sow good seeds, good things will find their way back to us."

"I often hear people say that they are waiting on their ship to come in. I ask them a simple question, have they sent one out?" Here's a warning, don't look for something to happen if you have not placed the circle into motion. The law of physics state that for every action there is an equal and opposite reaction. That is in line with the Law of the Circles, which states, what you give you get and what you sow you reap. But remember that you might sow only a little and it can multiply itself again and again, just like a kernel of corn will produce a stalk with ears of corn that are full of kernels. And I will always remember the words of Ralph Waldo Emerson as given to me by the Q-Bugs. "The creation of a thousand forests is in one acorn." I'm telling you this from the depth of my soul to communicate to you that it is all about the circles."

The space coach slowed dramatically and all aboard noticed the sudden change.

"We are here." Jill said with widened eyes as they all began to peer through the windows at the going-ons on the Planet of Dark Circles.

CHAPTER TWENTY-FOUR
The Darkest Circle

"I am going to have to get real deep with the happenings of this very dark place." Bill stated in a very matter-of-fact manner. "I will give many quotes that the Q-Bugs gave to me earlier. Jill and I did an awful lot of research in this area, because we really wanted to and we continually want to help those who are caught up in this vicious and dark circle known as domestic violence."

"Jill and I have a strong belief or theory on how healthy and unhealthy relationships develop to the extent that they encounter extreme and even lethal violence. Jill has agreed to talk to you about her theory sometime in the near future, but I will tell you about mine now. I reached this conclusion only after a comprehensive review of literature on the subject of domestic violence, along with interviews and observations. My theory relates to those key elements that may contribute to and hold positions of prominence in giving impetus to and maintaining the pattern of abuse in the domestic violence process or circle."

"Domestic violence to some degree, at least in an unhealthy relationship, is the result of insecurities and competition. Let me

301

begin by speaking to you on the subject of competition. Initially, there is competition by the male with other males for the female's attention. This is something of which we are all aware. This occurs in the early stages of both a healthy and unhealthy developing relationship. However, at some point, in the unhealthy relationship, the male begins to compete against the female. This is known as interpersonal partner competition. Let's go back to the onset of the relationship. Initially, the competition for the female is similar in both the healthy and unhealthy styles, but the competition ceases once closeness is established in the healthy relationship. Closeness occurs when the male sees himself as having won the affection of the female, and holding a position of uniqueness. They see themselves more as a couple than separates. In a healthy relationship, the interactions progress from a stage of competition to a stage of cooperation or the cooperative stage. In this stage, trust, love, and honesty emerge in an environment of mutual respect."

"Katherine Billie (1998, p. 14) states that the way a couple responds in interpersonal competition is an indicator as to whether the "relationship is headed for serious commitment or a bitter breakup." Sanders and Suls (1982, p. 721) hold that "Overall, it appears that spouses can be affected substantially by intra-marital comparison and competition, indicating that these forces may have a disruptive effect on the sense of unity produced by intimacy."

This competition can work both ways, which is to say that females may also compete for the attention, time, position, etc. of the male with other females. However, my focus here is on the male abuser. This is the case because he is the absolute principal perpetrator of abuse in the area of domestic violence. And because it is the male who for the most part abuses and kills his intimate partner or spouse, this issue is being addressed from the male-to-female perspective."

"Messman and Mikesell (2000, p. 21) state, "Competition in interpersonal interaction is inevitable." With this in mind, there is a need to understand that there will be competition, especially in the early phases of all relationships, as indicated by the drawings that appeared on the screen inside the coach, which are reflected in figures number one and two. Both figures are presented in an effort to illustrate what respectively comprises a healthy and unhealthy relationship. In block one we see that the male usually initiates this process by attempting to gain the attention of the female who is the object of his desire. This could be through a self-introduction; introduction by a mutual friend or he may choose from a myriad of other possible approaches."

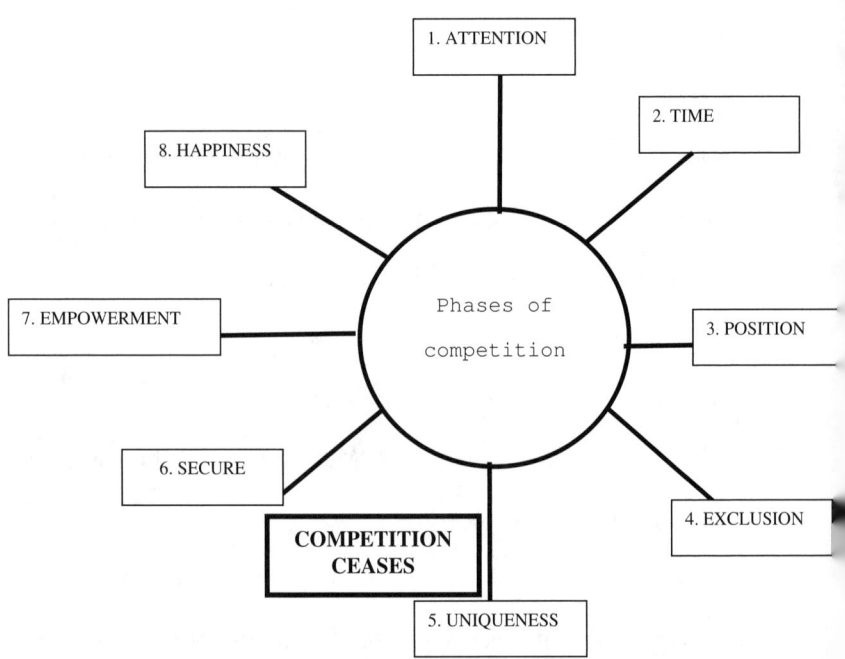

Figure one (Alberty's competitiveness in a healthy relationship)

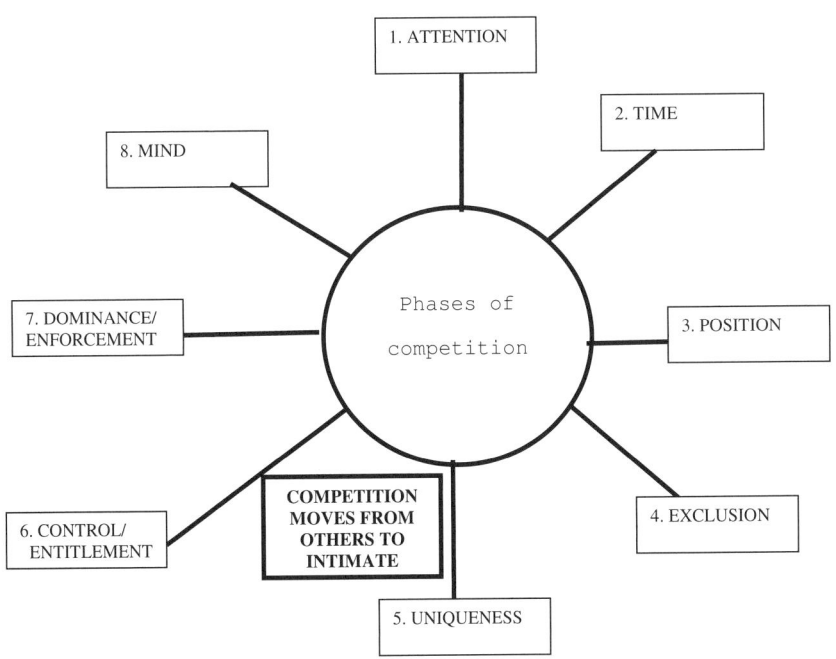

Figure two (Alberty's competitiveness in an unhealthy relationship)

In the next phase or block two, he attempts to increase and control the amount of time that he spends with her. This can be time in person, over the telephone, Internet chatting, etc. The purpose here is to ultimately become the prominent or significant figure in her perceptual world. The utilization of this time has as a clear goal, which we find in block three. It is the careful and determined jockeying for position. He wants to be the most prominent male that she cares for as a "boy friend, special friend, soul mate, or some other relative title."

"Hopefully, it is clear that this competitiveness for her attention, time and position all have the same common goal, which is control. In the article, "Competition and combativeness in courtship: Reports from men," Laner (1989, p.47) writes, "Competitiveness is seen as a direct measure of efforts to exert control." This position is not new."

In an earlier article (Shulman & Peven, 1971, p. 28) competition is defined as "striving to impose one's will."
This purpose of control or the imposition of one's will, moves the male to the next phase in block four, which is to have the female exclude all competing suitors from her social list. The male urges this exclusionary process until he feels that he sits in a position of

uniqueness. A point to note here is that some males not only want to exclude all competing suitors, but all males period. This can be an early sign that serious trouble lies ahead."

"This uniqueness is spoken of in the common vernacular as, "I am the only boyfriend and soon to be husband" or "I am the husband to the exclusion of all other males." In the healthy relationship where closeness is attained, competition ceases or is experienced only on a friendly or light basis. The definition of closeness can be refined to include, a merging of beliefs, values, and goals to the point that the two individuals perceive or see themselves more as a couple rather than two separates."

Bill emphasized. "It is important that the competition stops at this point. "Competition is exclusively negative in close relationships" (Messman & Mikesell, 2000, p. 21). If the competition continues, the relationship can be negatively affected. "Spouses can be affected substantially by intramarital comparison and competition, indicating that these forces may have a disruptive effect on the sense of unity" (Sanders & Suls, 1982, p. 721).

In a healthy relationship, the couple moves to the next phase in block six of seeing themselves as secure. Their activities are geared toward empowering themselves and one another, which moves them to block seven. As they become more empowered, they experience a sense of well-being and happiness as indicated by block eight. "Married people tend to take joy in spouses' achievements and empathize at losses, according to Steven Beach, Ph.D., and his colleagues at the University of Georgia" (Billie, 1998, p. 14).

"However, when this healthy relationship is compared to the unhealthy relationship, competition does not cease after block five. Instead it continues in the unhealthy relationship beyond the phase of acquiring uniqueness. The male not only competes for the female, but he now competes against her. He never really reaches phase six of security. He therefore, in his insecurity, attempts to exert further control over the female in a struggle for power and control. In essence, one can say that the struggle is for power, because he who has the power governs the levers of control. "The research on violence in marriages has focused attention on the power aspects of marriage. In an unpublished dissertation, Rushe analyzed marital transactions in terms of power and control strategies and concluded that the violent marriage is basically engaged in a power struggle" (Gottman & Notarius, 2000, p. 936).

"It is in phases six through eight, in the unhealthy relationship, that competition has a greater propensity for leading to episodes of serious interpersonal conflict or domestic violence. As the male presses to exert the control that he feels that he is entitled to, and where the female does not adhere to concede to such entitlement, a recipe for violence is created. In an effort to gain control, the male may try isolating her from her family and friends. This could mean moving to a different state or city."

"This may also come with demands of limited use of the phone in an effort of moving her mentally away from family and friends, as well as physically. One needs only to refer to a quotation from Hamptom and Gelles to understand this behavior, (1994, p. 109) which stated that there "were higher cases of domestic violence associated with those who had recently moved." The male in this unhealthy relationship might daily demand an account of what was done by the female by asking her questions like where did she go; what did she do; what took her so long; or scrolling through her cell phone looking at calls received, made, and missed. The purpose here is for the male to further gather information so that he can use it to justify the exertion of even more control over the female, while also justifying this abusive behavior to himself."

"If the female continues to resist being controlled or subject to the male's desire for power, he will systematically press more and more, even through violent confrontations, for such control. "The power dimension of violence suggests a systematic use of violence to intimidate and control the abused wife, instead of periodic uncontrolled outbursts" (Gottman & Notarius, 2000, p. 933).

"Should the female submit at this phase, the male, who will enforce his will with very little discretion, will begin to dominate her as indicated in block seven. In these unhealthy relationships, when females attempt to hold on to control of their lives and not submit their will to that of their abusive partners or spouses, the abusers feel that they have less power and will attempt to exert their will through more frequent displays of abusive behavior. "Within the domestically violent group, husbands who had less power were more physically abusive toward their wives" (Gottman & Notarius, 2000, p. 933).

"If the female does submit in phase six in the unhealthy relationship and progression to phase seven occurs, the male will then develop more fully these feelings of general dominance paired with his accompanying actions of enforcement, known as intimate terrorism, (IT) and will feel a sense of strong possessiveness or ownership over the woman. "The basic pattern in intimate terrorism is one of violence as merely one tactic in a general pattern of control. The violence is motivated by a wish to exert general control over one's partner" (Johnson & Ferraro, 2000, p. 949).

"It is at this point that fatalistic or lethal behavior becomes a strong possibility, unless the woman extricates herself or is extricated from this relationship by others. Even this must be coupled with the inability of the male to suspect her of the impending estrangement or to locate or discover her whereabouts once she has extricated herself from the relationship. "Several factors that often precede the killing of a woman by a man are a history of abusing, threats to kill her, unsuccessful attempts by the woman to exit the relationship in the past, prior criminal justice system contacts, and feelings of possessiveness or ownership of the woman on the part of the batterer" (Swinford, 2001).

"The male at this point is so controlling and domineering that he angers when the female does not do even his unspoken will. He now operates as if she is supposed to be able to read his mind as indicated in block eight. "Why didn't you cook?" he demands.

However, he is very seldom satisfied with even the most logical answer. "Didn't you know that I was going to be hungry?" (He asks this as if she could read his mind when more often than not, in the past, he ate before coming home). In reality he seeks to control not only her behavior, but also her thoughts, or at least control the way she thinks. He wants to give her the impression that he can read her mind in such a way as to imply to her, "You better not even think about: someone else; going against what I say; or ever leaving me."

"In this phase, in attempting to control the female's mind, the male may have her to dress to his unspoken expectations. These expectations will be expressed if nonconformity is noted. She may have to dress in a certain manner that he dictates. This could deal with the selection of colors that do not attract the attention of other males. She may have to choose clothes that are large enough so that they do not cling and highlight any feminine features. She may have to choose dresses that are long enough for his standards. This could mean that both the sleeves and the general length of the dress are sufficient to minimize the exposure of her arms and legs."

"She may have to clean the house by a certain time and to his specific standards. The standards could change daily to suit his purpose, which is control and dominance. He has made it clear to her that she is not to talk on the telephone. This of course is because the phone may be busy when he calls, and certainly she should know exactly what time he is going to call, though he never or very seldom tells her. His purpose and goal is to the greatest extent possible, to minimize any influence over her by others."

"Once this unhealthy relationship progresses to the point where attachment has taken place, it is extremely difficult for the female to safely extricate herself from the relationship. This type of male possesses what Dutton et al. (1994, p. 1370) refers to as a fearful and preoccupied attachment pattern. These individuals "are prone to the experience of anxiety about abandonment in their intimate relationships and, therefore, these attachment patterns are expected to be positively related to anger, jealousy, and affective instability."

"It would logically follow that if total control is the ultimate goal of the male in this unhealthy relationship, the contrasting extreme to this would be no control or either the perception or threat of no control. At this point, "no control" on the male's part exists when the female leaves or estranges herself from him or he perceives that she is planning to do so. This is an important point to note because the potential for severe violence, even to the point of lethal force, is now peaking as a real and viable option to this controlling and dominating male."

"In their study of 551 femicides, (where men kill women) Crawford and Gartner (1992, p. 44) concluded that "the offender's anger or rage over the actual or impending estrangement from his partner typified 45% of the cases where a motive could be established. In another 15% of cases the motive was the offender's suspicions about his partner's relationship with another man" (Crawford & Gartner, 1992).

"This is extremely significant. Statistics reveal that in 60% of the cases, where a motive can be determined, either actual or impending estrangement or the suspicion of a partner's relationship with another male, lethal violence was used against the female. In either case the motivating factor was the fear that the male had of losing control of the female or his perceived proprietary rights over her."

As Izzy and Lizzy looked around the Planet of Dark Circles, they could not believe their eyes. There was chaos and suffering everywhere.

"Why does this place even exist?" Lizzy asked.

"It wouldn't be nearly so populated if people were more courageous." Jill answered.

"Courageous?" Izzy asked curiously.

"Yes courageous." Bill answered. "If more neighbors would report abuse; if more doctors would report suspicious injuries of women; if more police officers were better trained to detect the signs of abuse and had mandated standard operating procedures for responding to both perceived domestic violence and actual domestic violence; if more politicians had the courage to pass laws that would protect women proactively rather than passive laws that in fact say that the male abuser must abuse or even murder before interdiction can occur, which all of us know is so often forever too late."

"How do we deal with this problem?" Lizzy tone and her wrinkled brow displayed a seriousness that had seldom been seen in her.

Jill responded. "We must all join groups that are actively working to effect positive change. We must do our part in reporting and educating others in our society who have the power to effect change for the better through laws."

The space coach suddenly moved quickly away from the Planet of Dark Circles. The sights had left them all emotionally and somewhat physically drained.

"I realize that a lot of this is hard to deal with, but this is the only way to get the large amount of information over to you in the short period of time that we have together."

"You know what they say, Bill added, "Λ picture is worth a thousand words, and if that is true then live observations must be worth at least 10,000 words." The journey was over almost as quickly as it had begun, but it had seemed an eternity. Izzy and Lizzy were again alone to ponder what they had heard and witnessed on the Planet of Dark Circles.

CHAPTER TWENTY-FIVE
The Amazing Circle of Planets

"Are you guys ready?" Jill asked.

"Yes." A robust Izzy and Lizzy answered. The Info-Bugs informed us that you would be coming by, and as usual you are right on time." Izzy smiled as he looked at his watch.

They were soon under way to the first planet of the Amazing Circle of Planets. "We were told that we were going to a place called the Amazing Circle of Planets. How did it get that name?" Izzy questioned.

"The planets in this particular system that we are visiting are all in a perfect circle around their sun. Each planet is the exact same distance from the sun and they are the exact same distance from each other; forming a perfect circle around the sun. It is simply amazing."

As they entered the solar system of the Amazing Circle of Planets, Lizzy pointed at a large purple planet outside of the window and asked, "Are we going to visit that planet?"

"No." Bill quickly responded. "That is the planet of ignorance and no lessons can be learned there."

"What's that planet?" Lizzy called out. It is the Amazing Children Planet. As their vessel entered the atmosphere of the Amazing Children Planet, Izzy and Lizzy immediately noticed and commented on the fact that everyone there was happy. Cheerful songs could be heard all around them.

"It is great that everyone is so happy, but why?" Izzy inquired.

"It is like that, because they truly are happy." Jill answered. "Most importantly they all still dream. Too often as adults we lose the ability to dream. I mean the types of dreams that say I can do anything and you not only go to sleep believing it, but you wake up believing it. It becomes a way of life for you. Yet they don't just dream."

"They don't?" Izzy challenged.

"No they do not." Jill interjected. "Notice that each of them have different color suitcases and various other carriers."

"Yes, I was trying to figure out why they all carried those things." Lizzy commented.

"Those things are plans." Bill answered.

"Plans?" Izzy Responded.

"Yes plans." Jill laughed. "Dreams are no good without plans that are implemented. They all have copies of their many plans. Some are already being implemented on other planets. Every one of these children and young adolescents will mature to do great things if they do not allow others to steal their dreams."

"Steal their dreams?" Lizzy thought aloud.

"Yes. Always there will be people who cannot dream; and others who are too afraid to dream; and still others who refuse to dream. These people must not be allowed inside of your circles. If you have people in your circles who belittle your dreams, who do not believe in your possibilities, and who are nay-sayers to everything that you say about your own personal growth; get them out of your circles immediately."

"Who are the ten individuals sitting around that large K and what does it stand for?" Izzy blurted.

"The K stands for knowledge. They are specialists at imparting knowledge to others on how to achieve. The Elder with the large diamond in his hand, and sitting in red apparel is the dreamer himself." Bill explained.

"It is so important that we follow our dreams." Jill added. "Langston Hughes wrote, Hold fast to dreams, for if dreams die, life is a broken winged bird that cannot fly."

"Remember." Bill spoke sadly. "It is said that the riches field in any town is the graveyard."

"The graveyard?" A surprised Izzy retorted.

"Yes." Bill continued. "It often has thousands of buried dreams, that had they been implemented, would have turned the world upside down in a positive and phenomenal way." When we have departed this life, so have our dreams, if we did not act upon them. After you're gone, you don't get a second chance to put your dreams into actions."

"This is one of those lessons that you have to get right the first time." Jill sighed. "If you do not fully understand what I am referring to, just ask the baby eagle about its first flight. It has to be right the first time or there is no second time."

Immediately they were approaching another planet. "What is that planet called?" Izzy questioned.

"It's called the Planet of Life and it is certainly not a very pleasant place." Jill continued as they hovered just above what appeared to be a huge and massive monster-like creature.

"Wow. Do you see that?" Lizzy exclaimed as she looked at the monster.

"How can we miss it?" Bill answered. "That monster is renowned. His name is Life. Life doesn't give up anything. He doesn't take anything; and he does not play. Most people think that Life owes them something. Those are the ones that he rips to pieces. Listen, you have to take and demand of Life what you want. He does not willingly give up anything. But know this that Life will give up its treasures only to those who are prepared to deal with Life on his terms. He does not compromise; cannot be bargained with; and has mercy on no one. So you must deal with Life from a position of strength or he will chew you up and spit you out."

"Who does life consider the weakest ones and easiest targets?" Asked Izzy.

"Oh that question is real simple to answer." Jill stated. "It's people who will not get started and quitters." Both she and Bill said simultaneously. "And next to those are the people who continually make excuses. Life exploits this knowledge about people and uses it to know who will be formidable in fighting for his treasures; or who will be weak and easy to destroy. Life knows that everyone is committed. They are either committed to their success, or they are committed to their failure. It is that simple. And it is really not that difficult to determine which ones win and which ones become Life's dinner. The winners are those who have a vision. They plan wisely; implement those plans with definitive time lines; and stick to the task until it is finished." Jill concluded.

Buzz came the Q-Bugs. "Consider the postage stamp; Its usefulness consists in the ability to stick to one thing 'til it gets there. Josh Billings. "

Buzz, quickly came another set of Q-Bugs, "Some men have thousands of reasons why they cannot do what they want to, when all they need is one reason why they can. Dr. Willie R. Whitney"

Buzz, quickly came even another set of Q-Bugs, "The check and balance rule of starting and finishing is do not start something, if it is not worth finishing; and especially know that you do not have to finish something that was never worth starting."

322

Unaware that the Q-Bugs had ever been there and that they had been frozen in position as the Q-Bugs made their quotes to Izzy and Lizzy, the Special Ones continued speaking without missing a beat. "You do not want people who will not start on their plans, procrastinators; and people who will not finish their plans, quitters; in your circles. You will have many sleepless nights if they are." Bill confided. "The motto of those that endure to the end is simple." He continued. "It is what the oak tree cries out in the middle of a raging storm. "If I am strong enough, long enough, this too will pass."

"I like that!" Izzy exclaimed and then repeated the words again. "If I am strong enough, long enough, this too will pass. Wow." Izzy reflectively pondered the words in relationship to his own life.

"For the strength of the oak tree, you have to reach way down deep within yourself." Lizzy whispered to Izzy as she softly held his hand and looked deep within his eyes. "Izzy, I remember my grandmother's words when I was like that oak tree. I mean when my storm came and I felt that I could not go on. She would say, Lizzy listen honey. You are going to have to be stronger than your storms; and to do that you must discover that there is more strength inside of you than you are aware of. She was talking about a "more" that I did

323

not even know existed. But it did. And somehow, in the remote parts of my soul, with my grandmother's encouragement, I made it through the darkness of my situations and found that elusive entity called "more."

The look on Izzy's face made it apparent that his mind was somewhere else. "Hello." Lizzy called out jokingly.

"Oh my, I'm sorry. Izzy apologized. "I don't know what happened." Izzy continued softly to Lizzy, obviously somewhat embarrassed. "I had a mind-warp back to a sad moment in my life. And I momentarily got stuck there." Izzy had been reflecting on the lost of his own grandmother, who was instrumental in guiding him through some very difficult times. Somehow Lizzy recognized that the mention of her own grandmother had triggered an emotional deluge in Izzy.

After getting a grip on his emotions, Izzy looked back on that part of his life more positively. He whispered. "My grandmother wasn't the only good person in my life. I have the best mother that anyone could imagine. She taught me something about storms too. She said, in the midst of your darkest storm, God is still God, with no less power to protect you."

They briefly embraced and smiled in their knowledge of the peace that they brought to each other. Their relationship indeed was very special. The peace they shared was more valuable than anything that either of them possessed.

WHO'S IN YOUR CIRCLES

CHAPTER TWENTY-SIX
Another Name for the Lands of Circles

Several weeks after returning from the Planet of Dark Circles, Izzy and Lizzy continued to reflect on the pain that people imposed on each other and allow to be imposed upon themselves. They had earlier learned that there were three more inner circles that people could reach in their very special relationships with one another and the Intimate-Self Circle. Those circles were the Land of the Intimate Circles and the Land of the Intimate-of-Intimate Circles. Their terrible observations on the Planet of Dark Circles helped them to better understand the severity of the pain that could infect and destroy the innermost circles of those who are not vigilant.

"Do you ever think that we will reach the intimate circles of the Special Ones?" Lizzy asked Izzy.

"I believe that with time and being faithful close friends, that all things are possible. I don't think that it should be something that we should focus on. If it is right then it will happen." Izzy replied.

"Of course, I know that you are right." Lizzy confessed after some thought. "But I must admit that I really enjoy their company. And I also believe that they truly enjoy ours."

327

"We certainly do." Jill said as she and Bill approached. "I am sorry, but we could not help overhearing you. Experience is the greatest teacher and time discloses almost all things. And this has taught us that there are rare lessons that are taught by experience only, while other lessons are only taught by time. Time has three parts on a streaming continuum. They are the past, present, and future. Sadly, too many people spend enormous amounts of time with regrets about their past and spend too much of their life forces focusing on yesterday's could haves, would haves, and should haves."

"Then there are those who are overly concerned about their future and waste too much of their life forces on tomorrow's potential problems or successes. Yet these moments of today are pregnant with unlimited possibilities that are rarely experienced by either of these individuals. While they look backward and forward, their precious todays eventually become more regrets of unfulfilled opportunities in their past. It is imperative that today must be lived today, one moment at a time."

"Though the future is truly a prepared place for those who prepare for it; they must prepare in such a way that they do not miss living the moments of each day."

Listen Bill continued. "This is an ancillary lesson to impress upon you "The Power of a moment." You must, as often as you can, live in the moment and squeeze all of the life and energy from it that it has. Remember that you deserve to be happy. Squeeze joy, hope, love, peace, happiness and all of the positive forces that you can from each and every moment. This is extremely important because, there is only one moment, one pulse, one breath, and one God, between life and death. Therefore populate your circles with people who embrace the philosophy of THE MOMENT." In a rich atmosphere of profundity, Bill and Jill then enjoyed tea and crumpets with Izzy and Lizzy. And then after a brief departure, Bill and Jill returned. It was now time for the next lesson.

"We have come to teach you another very important lesson that will bring clarity to why it should be difficult to move into the Friend, Close Friend, Intimate, and Intimate-of-Intimate Circles. We need you to take a walk with us." Bill said as he and Jill led the way.

The trip had been long and challenging. Bill and Jill seemed to make it with such ease, but Lizzy and Izzy were growing tired.

"Are you guys alright?" Jill asked as she stopped after noticing Izzy and Lizzy laboring in their breathing.

"We're fine, but I must admit that a little rest and a little water couldn't hurt right about now." Izzy smiled as he made his way to a nearby stone and sat on it along side Lizzy.

"That can easily be arranged." Jill responded. She pointed to a crystal clear spring just ahead in a clearing.

"The water there is ice cold and it tastes great." She said with a comforting smile.

"We can bring it to you." Bill offered.

"No we can make it that far." Lizzy softly laughed while looking at Izzy."

"Yes we can." Izzy smiled. "Yes we can." He repeated as he led the way.

Soon they were all taking long deep swallows of cold, clean, clear water. "This is amazing." Lizzy said with water dripping from her mouth onto her blouse.

"I love it." Izzy expressed between gulps, while lying on his stomach.

"Now let's get to the business of why we have made this long and challenging trip." Bill remarked as he stood and made his way to the front of a sign that marked the end of their journey. The sign said Land of Close Friends.

Izzy and Lizzy stared at the sign for awhile, before asking. "Is it possible that this sign has something to do with why we have come so far?"

"It has everything to do with why we have traveled out here." Jill answered.

"Info-Bugs." Billed called out.

"Info-Bugs at your service sir." It was Harry and the gang. They had about forty other Info-Bugs with them.

"We need you to remove this sign for just a moment and then put it back up." Jill requested.

"Sure." Harry said. Before he could get the word out of his mouth, about five of the Info-Bugs had already removed the sign. They gave it to Bill and waited and watched as Bill took the sign and placed it in Izzy's hands.

Izzy took the sign and read it again and again along with Lizzy until he finally said, "I am sorry, but I just don't get it."

"Turn the sign over and look at the back of it." Jill directed and then waited for a response from Izzy and Lizzy.

"What does this mean?" Lizzy asked as she saw the letters MV positioned next to each other on the reverse side of the sign.

"It refers to the other name for the Lands of Circles." Bill and Jill stated in unison.

"What other name? We never knew that the Lands of Circles had another name." Both Izzy and Lizzy confessed in earnest.

Jill looked at Bill with a long piercing stare. And after a deep sigh she softly, but emphatically stated, "MV is on the back of every sign that is at the entrance and exit points of all lands in the Lands of Circles. It stands for More Vulnerable. But it might as well be MP for more pain."

"Yes." Bill interjected. "The Lands of Circles is also known as the Circles of Vulnerability."

"But why?" Izzy questioned.

332

"Because the closer you allow others to move toward your intimate self, then the more vulnerable you become to the possibility of being injured by them." Jill answered.

"This is because as they move deeper inside of the circles, we share more sensitive and more personal information with them about ourselves." Bill added.

"It is for this very reason that you do not allow anyone into your inner circles without a great deal of observation and forethought. To go contrary to this is foolishness. There is no other way to say it." Declared Jill.

It was only after Bill and Jill left, that Izzy and Lizzy had time to reflect on their extraordinary and special relationship. Bill and Jill had made themselves vulnerable to Izzy and Lizzy. But Izzy and Lizzy also realized that they too had done the same thing with the Special Ones.

"You know, relationships, especially very close relationships are about trust and vulnerability. It's kind of scary when you think about the Planet of Dark Circles and the Planet Odium and all of the things that can go wrong. We must really think long and hard before we even remotely consider allowing anyone near our inner circles."

"Guess what I just thought about." Lizzy challenged capturing Izzy's attention. "I was thinking; it's true that the deeper we allow others into our inner circles, the more they know about us. And the more they know about us, the more vulnerable we become to being potentially injured by them. But also when it comes to vulnerability, we know more about ourselves than anyone else. Therefore, the person who is inside those inner most circles that can really do the most harm to us is ourselves. Ergo, we must take the time to know ourselves and investigate our own thoughts and the patterns of behavior that they give rise to."

"That is so true." Izzy pensively smiled. "We are the ones with the greatest potential of harming ourselves or for allowing others to harm us. I am impressed at your logic Lizzy." Izzy said with a broad smile. "The plot gets not only thicker, but deeper. The Lands of Circles are also the Circles of Vulnerability. Wow!"

CHAPTER TWENTY-SEVEN
A Poignant Departure

The next morning Izzy and Lizzy rose early to meet the sun as it kissed the sky good morning above the mountain ridge and rose to begin a brand new day. As they stood on the plush field of flowers, they reflected on all that they had experienced in this most wonderful place called the Lands of Circles.

Lizzy flung her hands into the air and twirled about with excitement as she cried out loudly, "This has simply been the most amazing place and the most awesome experience."

"Simply remarkable and astounding." Izzy enthusiastically confirmed. "I believe that the Lands of The Intimates, Intimate-of-Intimates, and Intimate-Self Circles that lie just ahead of us hold so many more wonderful experiences in store."

Suddenly from nowhere, a host of Info-Bugs appeared loudly exclaiming in unison, "You haven't seen anything yet!"

"What did they say?" Lizzy anxiously asked.

"They said that the journey has only begun." Izzy laughed loudly. "The journey has only begun!"

They happily rolled and frolicked in the field of flowers that inundated the hillside. Their laughter could be heard at a far distance. The sun was bright, the wind was cool and the birds happily sang their songs of cheer. Izzy and Lizzy paused in their excitement to see that even the old one-eyed owl was smiling from ear-to-ear.

"Maybe he remembered the butterfly." Lizzy laughed as she and Izzy rolled playfully in the grass. The freshness of their relationship had made them like children again; full of dreams and plans ready to be implemented.

With a tap on the shoulder, a voice rang softly into Dr. Ambrose's ear. "It is time to go now Dr. Ambrose."

"It's time to go?" He challenged in disbelief. It was difficult for Dr. Ambrose to withdraw himself from the Lands of Circles. It was even difficult for him to detect the gentle taps on his shoulder or recognize who the voice belonged to that was summoning him. It was Mr. Beacon his guide. Mr. Beacon carefully removed Dr. Ambrose's glasses of perception from his face. Reality quickly set in. A heartbroken Dr. Ambrose wanted desperately to immediately return to the Lands of Circles.

"But what about the journey to the other lands?" He protested.

"It is over Dr. Ambrose." Beacon said firmly. "Now you must write about your experience here so that others might learn. Now hold still." Mr. Beacon directed, as he placed his hand on Dr. Ambrose's forehead.

"What?" Dr. Ambrose said to himself as he quickly recognized the familiar setting of his office where he now sat in his oversized chair. It was not long before he was wondering if what he had witnessed had actually happened at all. Perhaps he thought; it was all a dream. But a new reality confronted him again as he noticed the ticket stubs from his plane tickets. They were on top of a small pamphlet that had written on it "Quick Tips from the Special Ones on Special Relationships." A note was attached to the pamphlet that promisingly said, "You Haven't Seen Anything Yet!"

"And so I, Dr. Ambrose, have written this book with the fastidiousness that Mr. Beacon instructed. I hope that it will alter your life for good. I know for a fact that the principles articulated within have personally changed my life forever! Oh by the way, I have attached the notes from the pamphlet of the Special Ones on the few pages that follow."

WHO'S IN YOUR CIRCLES

CHAPTER TWENTY-EIGHT
You Haven't Seen Anything Yet!

"You Haven't
Seen Anything
Yet!"

Quick Tips from the Special Ones on Special Relationships

Beacon

<u>Quick Tips for Those Preparing to Explore the Circles</u>

1. Be aware that we are **communicating all the time**. It is not just the words we speak that communicate. More than 70% of communication is non-verbal. We communicate in many ways: our eyes, our body language, posture, facial expressions, the way we dress, our proximity to each other, etc. Therefore it is very important to know how and what we are communicating to those in our circles, every circle.

2. WHEN we communicate is significant. **Timing is very important** in communicating to those in each of your circles. It is so important to establish effective communication patterns. One such pattern is to make sure to get the attention of the listener; their full attention. If not you will be frequently frustrated by the confusion that will follow. Choose to communicate at those moments when the other person is not intensely involved in something else. Respect their right to continue their involvement in what is important to them. Tersely put, learn to wait for the right moment or learn to create the right moment to communicate information that is important to you.

If we violate this rule of timing, what happens is a message is sent, but not received, because the attention of the listener is focused elsewhere. There are definitive signs of when the message is not received. We refer to this as the "No you didn't/yes I did" scenario. It's about what happens when we talk to someone without first getting their attention. You may have seen this scenario played out in your own life. Let us witness this "No you didn't/yes I did" scenario in the interactions of Vincent and Elizabeth that follows.

(The couple pulls into the parking lot of the civic center for the big event.)

Vincent: Hey Elizabeth, you did get the tickets didn't you?

Elizabeth: No, I thought that you had them.

Vincent: I did, but I put them on the table and asked you to put them in your purse.

Elizabeth: No you didn't.

Vincent: I did.

Elizabeth: No you didn't.

Vincent: Yes I did.

Elizabeth: No you didn't.

Vincent: Please just say that you didn't hear me, but do not tell me what I said or didn't say, I asked you to put the tickets in your purse.

Elizabeth: No you didn't.

Vincent: I know what I said.

Elizabeth: You must have thought you said it or maybe you said it to yourself or somebody else, but you didn't say it to me.

Vincent (insisting) I did.

Elizabeth: No you didn't.

Vincent: I wish I would have had a tape recorder running.

Elizabeth: Me too.

As you read this little example, it probably sounded really immature or childish. The reality is that we do sound childish when we go back and forth like this. When you hear the "No you didn't/yes I did" scenario or something similar, take this as a cue to listen more closely to what your significant other has to say. It simply means that the listener did not receive the message. And it says, in the future make sure that you have the listener's attention before speaking.

This is important because the listener could be in another conversation or maybe the listener is busy or preoccupied in thought. It could even be that you are talking in passing, and not really noticing that the listener is not receiving your message. At any rate get the listener's attention.

3. Another way that words can cause miscommunication is through using the word "you" inappropriately. When communicating with those in your circle, try to use "I" and "We" instead of "You" statements. When your partner hears "you" statements, he or she may feel that they are being accused and therefore assume a defensive posture. Imagine yourself in a courtroom where the prosecuting attorney is making accusations about the client for the defense. What does the defense attorney immediately begin to do? He or she begins to dissect what the prosecutor is saying and prepare their defense against it.

When your partner is being accused, or perceives that they are being accused, you can believe that their perception usually began with your "You" statements. And when they hear a "You" statement they too begin to prepare their defense. They stop listening and prepare for their own rebuttal to the initial part of the comments being made. So effectively communication has ceased. Now you only hear railing accusations that serves as avenues of destructiveness against the relationship.

4. **Blame** is a major cause of arguments in any kind of relationship within your circles. Simply said, **don't do it**. Blame is not about seeking resolution to the problem. Blame only looks for someone to make responsible or someone to be culpable for a wrong act.

5. **Don't Preach.** Leave the preaching to those in their pulpits and keep this destructive form of communication outside of your circles. Keep your issues short and simple. This is particularly the case when talking to immature individuals, which are usually, but not always children. In the era of AADD, ADD, and ADHD, many people's attention span will cause them to tune you out after only a short while.

6. K.I.S.S. (**Keep It Succinctly Short**) whenever possible, keep what you have to say brief and short. Do this even if it's nice and sweet.

7. Never make the mistake of **comparing your spouse** or intimate other with other people. This is even more important if you are doing this in a manner which says that the other person is better. This is a sure way of destroying the peace in any of the Lands of Circles.

8. Know that your **actions speak louder than your words**. Congruence in communication is when our actions match our words. When our words and actions do not match, most reasonable people will trust the actions rather than the words. Pay close attention to the

actions of those in your circles. Keep in mind that everyone, as the old adage goes, should "Practice what they preach."

9. **Do not talk too much** in your circle and do not allow people to remain in your circles who talk too much. Eventually they will get around to talking about you. There is a book that says, a fool speaks his entire mind; or put another way, a fool says anything that comes to his mind. And remember, a person that talks all of the time usually has very little to say.

10. It is very important to know that the only time that you have control over what is coming out of your mouth is before it comes out of your mouth. **Think before you speak**, it can save you a life of many regrets.

11. **Do not nag!** (Enough said)

12. **Be consistent.** Say what you mean and mean what you say.

13. Remember that **the tongue has the power** to build up or tear down. We may not want to hear this, but some of what we see standing in front of us in the person of our mates or intimate others, is what we have created with our own tongues. Create, encourage, empower and build up others with your tongue. Believe me, the

people in your circles, including yourself, need encouragement. So never underestimate the power of words.

14. **Don't interrupt** others while they are speaking. This can easily be interpreted to say that you feel that what you have to say is more important than what they have to say. It can even be said that you are saying that you are more important than the person that you are interrupting.

15. **Don't be condescending** or patronizing. This can really turn those in your circles off and totally block the channels of effective communication. And do not allow condescending or patronizing individuals to remain in your circles. The next person that they will soon be looking down their long supercilious nose at might be you.

16. **Hitting is never an option unless you're swinging at a baseball.** Physical and verbal abuse are extreme forms of disrespect. A man or woman, who abuses his or her mate or intimate other, communicates a most disdainful scorn for them as a person. Since more than 90 percent of reported abuse is male to female, allow me to address this to the women. If you **ALLOW** a man to start or continue to abuse you physically, emotionally or verbally, you communicate to him that you care more for him than you do yourself.

This communicates low self-esteem and low self-worth. And the associated guilt or shame of allowing such abuse against yourself only makes the situation worst. You are precious and extremely special, no one, and I mean no one should ever be allowed to put their hands on you in anger or speak to you abusively.

17. There will come times in relationships when there will be legitimate differences. These situations should be dealt with properly. When it does happen, remember to **never attack the other person's character**. Focus on the issue and the solutions to those issues and stay away from character references.

18. It is not just what you say, but most of the time it is how you say it. **Speak respectfully** and be sure that those that are allowed into your circles also speak respectfully.

19. Do not use absolutes when referring to those in your circles, especially those that are close to you. Do not use words like always, only, never, or phrases like all the time and every time. There are very few absolutes among human beings.

20. **Do not be a psychic or a mind reader,** and also do not expect your intimate others to be clairvoyant. Tell those in your circles clearly what you want them to know. Do not expect them to

understand your intimations, insinuations, and subtle hints and actions.

21. Discuss issues at a conversational tone. Do not allow loud and rude individuals to enter or remain in your circles. This is a serious issue of disrespect.

22. Do not bring up highly charged **emotional subjects** when you or those in your circles are weary, exhausted, or during tense or hurried times. Such discussions should be reserved for a mutually agreed upon time.

23. Unresolved problems grow and are fertilized by time. **Resolve differences as soon as possible** with those in your circles.

24. What you **don't say** is just as important as what you do say at times. If it is true, be willing to say: I'm sorry; I love you; I forgive you; I trust you. When you do not say these things, it could easily be construed that you are not sorry; you do not love, forgive or trust the other person who is experiencing these dynamics with you.

25. **Lighten up! (Enough said).**

26. **Contend fairly.** Do not bring up issues from the past that were earlier resolved between you and those in your circles. Throw away your shovels and stop robbing graves.

27. Did you know that in communicating with those in your circles, there is no such thing as a winner and a loser? Both parties must be either winners or losers. Think about it, I disagree with someone in my inner circles, and through wit and intelligence I put them to shame. I won, right? How can I be a winner, when my close friend or intimate other loses? That can only be the case in an unhealthy set of inner circles. We rise together, or we fall together. The operative word is "together."

28. Never forget that little things mean a lot. It was a little piece of foam that contributed to the demise of a space shuttle.

29. Remember when you are tempted to get even or retaliate, YOU ARE BETTER THAN THAT!

30. Share what you have learned with others. Send the book to them as a gift. It is the best way to help them understand your new behaviors.

WHO'S IN YOUR CIRCLES

REFERENCES

Billie, K. (1998). When couples compete. *Psychology Today,*
31, 14.

Crawford, M. & Gartner, R. (1992). *Women killing intimate*
femicide in Ontario, 1974-1990. Retrieved May 20, 2002,
from EBSCOhost Academic Search Elite.

Dutton, D. G., Saunders, K., Starzomski, A., & Bartholomew,
K. (1994). Intimacy-anger and insecure attachment as
precursors of abuse in intimate relationships. *Journal of*
Applied Social Psychology, 24, 1367-1386.

Gottman, J. M. & Notarius, C. I. (2000). Decade review:
Observing marital interaction. *Journal of Marriage &*
Family, 62, 927-947.

Hampton, R. L. & Gelles, R. J. (1994). Violence toward
Black women in a nationally representative sample of Black
families. *Journal of Comparative Family Studies*, 25, 105-
119.

Johnson, M. P., & Ferraro, K. J. (2000). Research on
domestic violence in the 1990s: Making distinctions.
Journal of Marriage & Family, 62, 948-967.

Laner, M. R. (1989). Competition and combativeness in
courtship: Reports from men. *Journal of Family Violence,*
4, 47-62.

McEwen B. S. (2005). Stressed or stressed out: What is the
difference? *Journal of Psychiatry Neuroscience*; 30(5) 315-
318.

Messman, S. J., & Mikesell, R. L. (2000). Competition and
interpersonal conflict in dating relationships.
Communication Reports, 13, 21-38.

No Author, (1985). *National Enquirer Conquering Stress*.

Romine, C. B., & Reynolds, C. R. (2005). A model of the
development of frontal lobe functioning: findings from a
meta-analysis. *Applied Neuropsychology*, 12, 4, 190-201.

Sanders, G. S., & Suls, J. (1982). Social comparison,
Competition marriage. *Journal of Marriage and the Family*,

44, 721-731.

Shulman, B. H., & Peven, D. (1971). Sex for domination. *Medical Aspects of Human Sexuality,* 5, 28-32.

Swinford, S. P. (2001). Understanding domestic homicide: Book review. Journal of Marriage & Family, 63, 279.

Appendix

Your contribution to this and the next book

SUBMISSION

Please write your thoughts on how this book has made your

relationship(s) more special.

_____

_____

_____

_____

_____

_____

_____

_____

_____

_____

I have written my personal experiences. I give the author of "_Who's In Your Circles and Why?_" exclusive rights to utilize what I have written and submitted to him in a revised edition of this book, or a sequel to this book, or in any way that the author so chooses in an effort to promote the concepts of this book. My words may be altered or truncated for space. I hold the author, publisher and all affiliates harmless. I understand that I will receive no payments or remuneration for my submission. I yield all rights to my submission to the author. I am at least 18 years or older. You may copy this form to make more than one submission. Send to Dr. John Alberty at   P. O. Box 82, Gracewood, GA 30812

_____   _____

   Signature   Date

Contact and Purchasing Information

Visit our website at: www.whosinyourcircles.com

To order from among our many other items please visit our website at www.whosinyourcircles.com

To order books by postal service, fill in the form below and mail with payment to P.O. Box 82, Gracewood, GA 30812

ITEM	PRICE	QUANTITY	TOTAL ITEM PRICE
BOOK	16.99		
GA residents add 7% sales tax	1.19		
Shipping and Handling in U.S. **USPO PRIORITY MAIL** **EACH ADDITIONAL BOOK** USPO REGULAR MAIL EACH ADDITIONAL BOOK	Select below 4.95 1ST BOOK 3.00 EACH 4.00 EACH 2.50 EACH		
Total			
Your mailing address: Name: _____ Address: _____ City: _____ State: _____ Zip: _____ Telephone: _____ Email address: _____			

☐ Check here if you want information on other books. You may find

information for booking Dr. Alberty at the website listed above. The

author would like to thank you ahead of time for your patronage.

Contact and Purchasing Information

Visit our website at: www.whosinyourcircles.com

To order from among our many other items please visit our website at www.whosinyourcircles.com

To order books by postal service, fill in the form below and mail with payment to P.O. Box 82, Gracewood, GA 30812

ITEM	PRICE	QUANTITY	TOTAL ITEM PRICE
BOOK	16.99		
GA residents add 7% sales tax	1.19		
Shipping and Handling in U.S. **USPO PRIORITY MAIL** **EACH ADDITIONAL BOOK** USPO REGULAR MAIL EACH ADDITIONAL BOOK	Select below 4.95 1ST BOOK 3.00 EACH 4.00 EACH 2.50 EACH		
Total			
Your mailing address: Name: _____ Address: _____ City: _____ State: _____ Zip: _____ Telephone: _____ Email address: _____			

☐ Check here if you want information on other books. You may find

information for booking Dr. Alberty at the website listed above.

The author would like to thank you ahead of time for your patronage.

A PLACE FOR YOUR NOTES

A PLACE FOR YOUR NOTES

WHO'S IN YOUR CIRCLES